Curriculum Speak;
Developing English for Academic Literacy

Premise
Academic English is vastly different from
day-to-day, social & personal expression.
Students need to be able to talk and write about ideas.
Educators need to identify and teach these skills.

Construct
Provide background research in language learning.
Identify specific learning challenges.
Present Activities that Build English Facility
with the Language Demands inherent in Content Units

How
Practical activities, sequenced in difficulty,
develop student English proficiency with
Vocabulary & Terminology
Pronunciation & Stress
Sentence Construction
Paragraph Discourse
Lengthy Discourse

Table of Contents

1	Curriculum Speak
3	Knowing Challenges
5	The Language Chasm
11	Pedagogy Informs Practice
16	Who is an English Language Learner?
17	Culture in Schooling
20	Negotiation for Meaning
22	Tolerance for Ambiguity
24	Comprehensible Instruction
25	Best Practice Approaches
27	Communicative Competence
28	Specific English Challenges
30	English Speaking Proficiency
38	Sentences Stress
44	Discourse Complexities
48	Cultural Dissonance
50	What is Your Function?
57	What Comes First?
64	Verbs; Cognition and Constraints
80	Identifying a Language Skill
83	Vocabulary Difficulties
84	Grammar Difficulties
85	Discourse Difficulties
86	Subject-Specific Difficulties
89	Instructional Challenges
91	How Do I Teach Language in Content?
95	Text Book Terrors
107	How to Check on Student Comprehension
112	Instructional Games and Activities
114	Activities and Games - Vocabulary
129	Activities and Games - Sentences
147	Activities and Games - Discourse
185	Language Buddies
193	Assessment: What and How
203	Internet Sites
204	Bibliography

Author's Note

I felt that educators needed a more practical and user-friendly resource to help implement the concept of teaching language skills alongside content instruction. The ideas in Curriculum Speak come from several sources. The first is my teaching experience, my continuous need to bond speaking with literacy for students.

Secondly, I derived my focus on this language continuum, 'word-sentence-paragraph-subject-specific-discourse' from my tutoring work with a very clever (Einstein) Grade 9 student from Taiwan. Daniel is so bright, so multi-talented and has these amazing interpersonal skills that draw people in so they recognize his social nature and appreciate his talents, intellect, love of sports, superior art talent, and his truly wonderful sense of humour. Such was Daniel's experience through his first year in ESL class that he made many friends and superior grades. Then 'WHACK', Daniel's sense of his abilities, and his security in success hit a wall. The wall was in the form of grade 10 text book learning, specifically Civics, History and Science classes, and yes, English.

Daniel experienced tremendous trouble immediately and we had to cover the whole gamut from individual words, people's names, sentence intonation, lengthy sentences in paragraphs to discourse and text attack skills. It was as if this genius child from an advantaged background had suddenly suffered brain and language loss.

Third, while doing my research, I found this incredible list delineating language skills at the level of individual vocabulary items, sentence level skills and discourse, but I lost the source and therefore cannot reference the author. For that I solemnly apologize. That list galvanized my own work, and provided me with a middle ground between pedagogy and practice, where I could apply my belief that speaking and literacy go together even with beginners to English. So, the activities bond speaking with literacy, and no doubt would please Piaget for their appropriateness to student age and cognition, and the emphasis on student interest and involvement.

Although in 'Curriculum Speak' I started with practical activities for vocabulary, then sentences, et cetera, students learn language across different areas at the same time, so my language items are not a recipe where teachers "do this first, then that then . . . ". Remember, paragraphs and sentences provide the context for making sense of new vocabulary and when something makes sense to students, they will remember it better.

These are my goals for Curriculum Speak

1) to prepare teachers to recognize the content difficulties that students usually experience while learning English

2) to help teachers develop a professional skill set reflective of language learning, instruction and 'best practices'

3) to provide specific, practical activities that accomplish these

4) to guide teachers in authentic assessment better suited for ELLs as opposed to standard tests and marking schemes

Educators will find most of the activities work across grades and subjects. Build your own repertoire of language learning tricks by choosing activities that you feel most comfortable using and that your students will enjoy.

Curriculum Speak

'Curriculum Speak' is a series of speech-based activities which provide classroom and subject teachers with content-scaffolding activities that support English Language Learners (ELLs) in their acquisition of fluent speech and academic literacy.

The focus of these activities is twofold:
1. to improve student speaking proficiency
    - ✓ ELLs will become comfortable and confident when they speak English with partners, in groups or in front of their class or an audience.
    - ✓ ELLs will develop appropriate speech skills regarding pronunciation, syllable stress, intonation and emphasis, syntactic competence and discourse expertise.

2. to improve student success with academic curriculum
    - ✓ ELLs will be involved with multiple opportunities to develop expressive language skills using the words, functions, concepts and discourse styles of graded curriculum.
    - ✓ ELLs will learn language skills alongside subject matter in natural contexts.
    - ✓ ELLs will be successful in tests and exams.

Curriculum speaking activities in this guide benefit all students not only ELLs. Oh yes, and one more person! Teachers. It won't take long before teachers develop trust in the value of curriculum speak and consider them to be better scaffolds and instructional tools than any textbook or worksheet.

Terms Used in this Guide

ELL
English Language Learner

Scaffold Instruction
Instructional activities that support student learning with incrementally challenging tasks that build skills and knowledge

Modifications, Adaptations, Accommodations
Changes made to the presentation, procedures, text form and/or assessment strategies that help provide students with greater accessibility to successful learning

Authentic and Performance Assessment
Assessment procedures that rely on indicators of progress aside from test results, including reference to a student's starting point in skills, portfolios of work and conferencing sessions, and observations regarding a student's growth in behaviours such as social, attitudinal and confidence

Language Conscious Teachers LCT
Teachers attuned to ELL proficiencies in verbal fluency and literacy skills, who recognize probable challenges for ELLs, and who have the skills to structure requisite modifications enabling student success, at his/her levels

Knowing the Challenges Helps Educators Identify Student Needs

1. Language Learning Pedagogy
2. Specific English Challenges
3. Identifying a Language Skill
4. Instructional Challenges
5. Instructional Games and Activities
6. Assessment; What and How

Knowing the Challenges

1. Language Learning Pedagogy

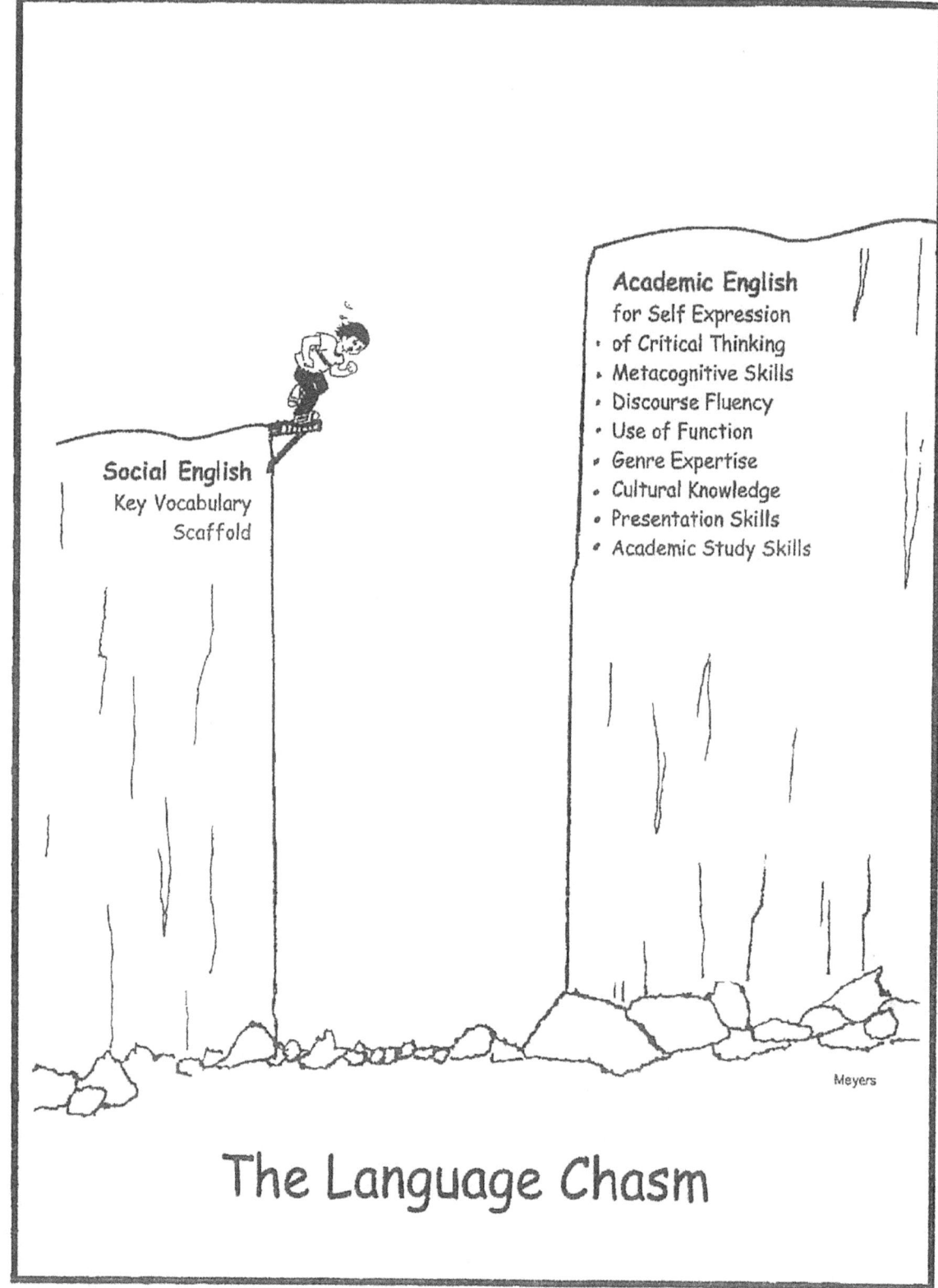
Curriculum Speak; Developing English for Academic Literacy

The Language Chasm

The What
What are the skills that language learners must have in order to attain academic proficiency?

The How
How can educators help their ELLs to learn those skills and to bridge the chasm to academic success?

The following sections will provide information about language acquisition and the challenges that face English language learners and their teachers.

Educators will become aware of skills that range along a language continuum, and then learn about strategies and activities that address the missing scaffolds depicted in 'the Language Chasm'.

Academic Literacy

On the one hand, academic literacy refers to the knowledge and use of overarching and metacognitive concepts such as

- ✓ Analysis
  (synthesizing, evaluating, bridging inference, delineating cause and effect, showing consequence, organizing pertinent information, detail and proof)

- ✓ Discourse competency in speech and written styles
  (in order to change opinion/ideas/action, explanations, experimentation, recording, informing, negating, negotiating, creating, stylistic and literary techniques)

On the other hand, academic literacy refers to specific knowledge and use of English language skills such as

- ✓ Cultural Competencies
  Linear thinking in a presentation
  (cultural worldview may affect thought and discourse style)
  Cultural relevance (accounts for audience norms, idiomatic language, historical and religious background)

- ✓ Speaking Skills
  Appropriate body language, eye contact and vocal techniques
  (intonation, phrasing, pausing, emphasis)

- ✓ Technological Literacies
  (using, searching, referencing, creating new technology(ies) for communication)

Pedagogy Informs Practices

- How Long Does it Take?
- The Retention and Development of First Language Skills
- Who are Your English Language Learners?
- Cultural Issues in Learning
- Negotiation of Meaning; Scaffolds
- Tolerance for Ambiguity
- Comprehensible Learning
- Best Practice Approaches for ELL
- Communicative Competence

How Long Does It Take?
Language Learning Backgrounder

It usually takes close to two years for students to learn basic communication skills in a new language. Professor Jim Cummins, from the University of Toronto's Modern Language Center, is a renowned expert in the field of language learning. Cummins confirms that students initially learn vocabulary, literacy and speaking skills for day-to-day situations within two years. On the other hand, he warns us that this basic communication stage is only the tip of the iceberg. Cummins' research proves that it could take students 7 years, or more, to develop competency in the many language skills requisite for success in higher grades.

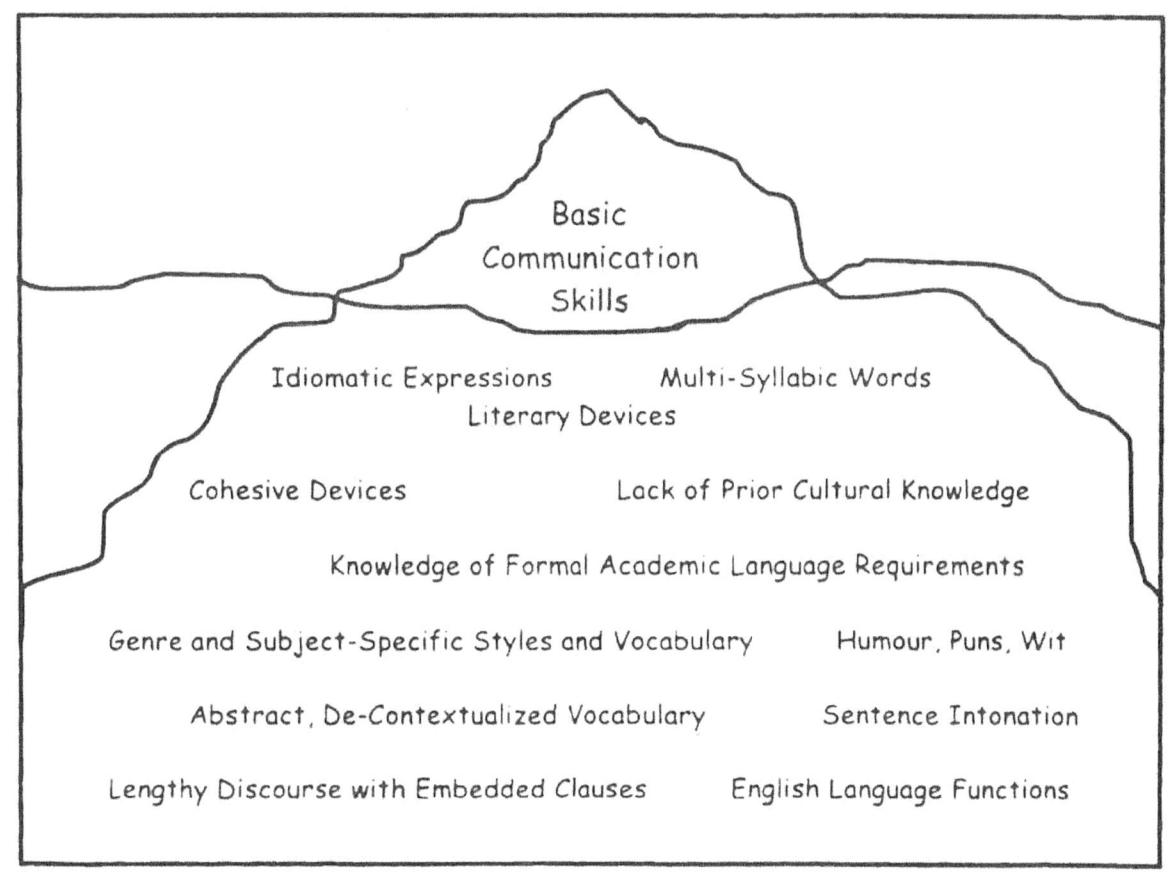

Step by Step, We Learn Vocabulary, Speaking and Literacy Skills to Develop Proficiency in English

"You speak English O.K. You're ready for regular class work. Good luck!"

Whew! This is hard.

It only took me 9 years!

① learning basic-level vocabulary for common objects, expressing needs, day-to-day tasks, and socializing

② starting to speak spontaneously, developing ability to use longer discourse on a known topic and with peers; developing a broader base of general vocabulary, improving pronunciation and intonation, just starting to compose in writing

③ gaining confidence and greater word knowledge to partake in class discussions, acquiring knowledge of verb tense, cohesive devices, and literacy conventions, although unable to apply this knowledge consistently in either speech or assignments

④ catching up on phonetic and word skills as well as improving literacy skills, developing an awareness and skill with the use of formal speech, English rules of politeness and appropriate language use required for speech and written tasks

⑤ improving cultural and linguistic knowledge, gaining skill with subject specific vocabulary and assignment expectations, growth of range of vocabulary

⑥ gaining improved fluency, comprehension and use of literate-type language skills, and various functions of English

⑦ idioms, analogy, similes, genre specific styles, alliteration, humor, lengthy discourse, native-like fluency

Critical Research into Language Learning

"There is a need for instruction that builds structural and semantic coherence", reaffirms Nanette Koelsch, Senior Research Associate at WestEd Research Institute, California. Koelsch chose to quote a report from the National Literacy Panel on Language-Minority Children and Youth* because researchers now recognize that teachers have to go beyond mere vocabulary instruction; they must teach a series of ever challenging skills along a language continuum. Knowledge of words and general English proficiency will not guarantee academic success.

This resource, Curriculum Speak, identifies the language skills continuum from vocabulary learning, sentence constructs and meaning, paragraph and text discourse, and subject-specific genres. Even better, Curriculum Speak provides practical activities and games for each level to guide educators in connecting those language skills to grade-required content instruction.

The Language Continuum

| Vocabulary | Phrase | Sentence | Discourse | Academic Literacy |

ELLs don't leap from vocabulary knowledge to communication via discourse and academic proficiency.

* Nanette Koelsch, 'Improving Literacy Outcomes for English Language Learners in High School: Considerations for States and Districts in Developing a Coherent Policy Framework' 2007, WestEd Regional Research Center, California, USA

# The Development and Retention of First Language Skills

Research points to the fact that skills in one language transfer easily and naturally to reflect similar performance in subsequent languages. Students who have well-developed first language skills, and who know themselves to be successful learners, will feel confident about their abilities to learn English.

Bi-lingual Education in primary grades is based on the belief that children have an advantage in learning if their home language is used to ensure that students develop a rich vocabulary, abstract concepts and higher-order thinking skills. Obviously, schools that offer no bilingual supports will not be as successful in enabling students in those areas.

In <u>Empowering Minority Students</u>, Jim Cummins describes educational approaches as being empowering or disabling, and as either additive or subtractive of culture and language. He argues that if educators see their role as one of replacing or subtracting students' language and culture so that they can superimpose English, then they are likely to disempower those children. On the other hand, encouraging children to use their home languages while they learn is a way to empower students.

The preceding information forms a powerful rationale for educators to encourage translation, and to use first language tutors for enrichment or remediation. Consider the strategies your own school has in place to empower families.

Home Language Use in English Immersion Classes

Should students use their home language in class?
Absolutely, yes!
How much translation is okay?
Whenever teachers or students feel the need.

When and Why?
- to acknowledge a student's identity and felt needs
- to ensure comprehension of concepts and events
- to translate necessities (fees, schedules, events)
- to enable parent-school communications
- to validate first language peer supports
- to encourage students to think and learn in the language in which they are most articulate

> A study from Margaret Early in Vancouver showed that middle school ELLs who were allowed to use their first languages in class to process an inital content task, scored higher on tests in English than their English speaking peers. Therefore, as long as the final product is always in English, allow translations.

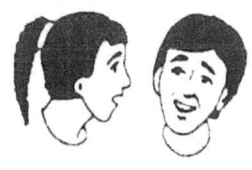

Who is an English Language Learner?
Classroom Data Regarding Home Language

1. Use a class list.
2. Beside each student interviewed write their answers to the following three questions.
3. Answers to questions 1 and 3 indicate the language most likely to be used in the home.

Questions
- a. What language did you use before you started school?
- b. What language do you speak at home now?
- c. What extra language is spoken in your home?

Implications
- Student is probably bilingual
- Student learns in both languages
- Home language will support the student's acquisition of abstract thinking skills
- Home language will support the student's cognitive development
- Teachers may ask students to get help from their parent(s) about a concept
- Teachers can encourage a student to use their first language (L1) to translate a word or idea in class

Culture in Schooling

It is difficult to be objective about one's culture because we are so imbued with its norms, rules and references that we assume everyone shares the same values and prior knowledge. In multiethnic communities, cultural expectations and beliefs often affect teachers as much as students. Consider the following.

> Example 1 – A grade 7 reading assignment is about rural Quebec teenagers in winter.
> Example 2 – During a primary unit on animals, a student asks if there are lions in our forests.
> Example 3 – Muslim sisters study in a small room while other students take gym, or dance.
> Example 4 – A mother turns up at the teacher's classroom door obviously embarrassed and apologetic. She wants to know what she has to do to help her son get ready for the Halloween party.
> Example 5 – Several students use the health room for prayers.
> Example 6 – Additional foods had to be added to the Food Guide.

Empowerment education requires educators to acknowledge and respect diversity, and still share North American cultural concepts, symbols, vocabulary, and expectations. Teachers cannot be expected to know everything about cultural differences, but we can encourage information sharing from students about special days, events, and traditions.

Language Conscious Teaching
Transitions - Culture Shock

The psychological, emotional and personal effects of living, learning, socializing and working in a new country is compounded when the culture, language, values, customs and society is very different from that of your own family and upbringing. The greater the disparity between an individual's prior worldview and the new society, the greater the impact of Culture Shock is felt.

There is general agreement amongst Humanistic Psychologists regarding the steps and effects involved in the process of acculturation. Recent research, moreover, is taking a more serious look at the consequences on individuals and groups in the area of mental health and the academic repercussions of Culture Shock.

There is a psychological cost of the loss of communication control, of disorientation, of being in a constant state of high stress, fearful and alert for non-verbal signs that give sense to new, incomprehensible situations. What a difference teachers and school reception practices can make to lower that discomfort!

Keep in mind that students acculturate to new environments at different rates, even amongst family members. In language training, there is a well-known stage called The Silent Period, in which students do not yet have the knowledge or confidence to risk speaking English in class. For certain students, this Silent Period may last a long time. Be encouraging and inclusive.

Please read the Stages in the Acculturation Process.
Share your own experiences in the whole group discussion.

Culture Shock and Acculturation

First Stage – Initial Enthusiasm
Newcomers may
- feel excitement, idealism, eagerness
- have some anxiety about the future
- feel optimistic about new opportunities and the new country

Second Stage – Culture Shock
Newcomers may
- experience confusion, misunderstandings and anxiety
- see themselves as observers
- feel depressed and isolated
- demonstrate withdrawal, alienation, and even aggressiveness
- avoid contact with the mainstream culture or community

Third Stage – Recovery
Newcomers may
- have more constructive attitudes and feel less anxious
- speak better English and understand more
- try new behaviours and test limits

Fourth Stage – Integration
Newcomers may
- feel that their emotional equilibrium is restored
- show trust and humour
- be able to value both the old and new culture

Negotiation for Meaning

Renowned ELL researcher, Stephen Krashen talks about the process where people try to understand each other, to communicate, to clear up mistakes or confusion. He called this dance of give and take the 'negotiation of meaning'.

The clearest example of negotiation of meaning occurs within newcomer instruction. It is easy to see attempts to convey meaning with basic level language learners. Some examples are

- Vocal efforts to approximate a word or phrase
- Eye/facial expressions of confusion or encouragement
- Vocal expressions of confusion or encouragement
- Miming
- Gesturing for emphasis or meaning or frustration
- Drawing, writing
- Using the unknown language to explain/express
- Speaking louder, stressing key words
- Re-trying with the addition of one/many of the above ideas
- Use of a translator or bi-lingual dictionary

When ELLs have greater facility with English, the strategies for negotiation of meaning are more complex, and instead of speaking about 'attempts' at meaning-making, educators use the terms 'scaffold/scaffolding'. Scaffold strategies include those above, but add tactics like re-wording, contextualizing, using known expressions for further interaction, such as," Please repeat that.", "I still don't understand.", "Show me.", "Did you mean . . .?" Scaffolds include DVDs and other visuals, and graphic organizers.

Key Visuals Show Content Graphically

Posters

Timelines

Action Strip/Storyboard

Videos/Movies

Maps

Graphs

Outlines

1. a) _____
   b) _____
   c) _____
   d) _____
2. a) _____
   b) _____

Flow Chart - Cause and Effect

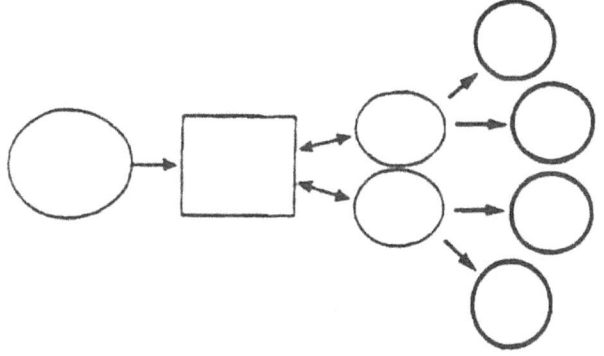

Tolerance for Ambiguity

Language learners at the Basic level are given a lot of assistance with language learning. Teachers simplify English vocabulary and grammar. Telegraphic type speech is accepted, and translation, visuals and interactive activities support students' comprehension.

As English lessons continue, students learn more and more vocabulary and complex structures. Grammar rules and literacy become more challenging. When this happens students often become confused and frustrated. Students become upset with their limitations and inhibitions in English. Some students feel anxious and overwhelmed; they have to make guesses and accept less than perfect results.

Teachers need to be aware of this phenomenon; it is called "Tolerance for Ambiguity". It occurs when students start to feel anxious and overwhelmed about comprehension and new language challenges. Some people have a greater tolerance for ambiguity. Confusion and frustration don't seem to bother them very much.

It is imperative that students regain self-confidence in their abilities. Therefore, if a teacher perceives students who are frustrated and seem unable to cope with language challenges, there are ways to help.

Tolerance for Ambiguity

- ✓ Give students a pep talk: praise their efforts and progress.

- ✓ Acknowledge the difficulties and challenges everybody has with language learning.

- ✓ Encourage students to risk a guess or make a mistake.

- ✓ Accept partial answers.

- ✓ Delay new lessons, and extra skills.

- ✓ Revert to using previous language activities and games.

- ✓ Focus on developing student confidence and success.

Note: When teachers begin to use textbooks and informational articles in English, they will need to use similar techniques to help students feel confident about such challenges.

Comprehensible Instruction

Stephen Krashen, a popular expert in language theory and training, tells educators that students will acquire a new language if it is comprehensible, that is, if they can understand it. Krashen adds that opportunities to practice using the new language are equally important. He calls these two crucial learning components 'Comprehensible Input' and 'Opportunities for Output'

Comprehensible input and opportunities to use English in speaking and writing are the foundations of language acquisition.

Krashen says that to ensure Comprehensible Input, language must
- ✓ be understood by the student
- ✓ be tied to the student's frame of reference (prior knowledge and experiences)
- ✓ be adjusted to the student's current language abilities
- ✓ match student cognitive and cultural backgrounds (age, maturity, intelligence, values, worldview)

Best Practice Approaches for Language Learning

> The Language Experience Approach
>
> Active Learning Approach
>
> Integrated Skills or Whole Language Approach
>
> Multiple Intelligences Approach
>
> Cooperative Learning Approach
>
> Thematic Learning Approach

The essence of ELL 'best practices':

- Talk is an essential aspect of learning
- A risk-free, supportive, interactive environment
- A variety of different sources of language models
- Multiple opportunities for comprehending information
- Multiple opportunities for expressing knowledge
- Implicit integration of four language skills
- Language learning tied to real contexts/content
- Linguistic and cultural empowerment

"Language codes the experience we are having."
Gordon Wells, The Meaning Makers

COMMUNICATIVE COMPETENCE

- **Linguistic Competencies**

  These involve knowlege of
  - the vocabulary,
  and
  - the grammar rules (structure) of the new language.

- **Socio-linguistic Competencies**

  These involve knowing the appropriate
  - social rules of language (formality, directness, body language),
  - non-verbal behaviours in that culture, and when and where to use these behaviours.

- **Discourse Competencies**

  These involve the ability to make language connections, to understand the coherence of lengthy written or spoken contexts, through special linking words, inference, or rhetorical devices.

- **Strategic Competencies**

  These include the mastery of talk techniques: how to get into or out of conversations, break silences, hold the floor in conversations, handle communication breakdowns.

Communicative Competence

There are students who speak English but who are functionally illiterate. Then there are students who can read and spell English with some skill, but they are not conversant. There are also students who are competent in English speech and literacy but who feel they lack culturally relevant norms and social skills, called socio-linguistic competencies. Each of the afore-mentioned groups lacks particular English skills required for authentic communicative competence.

The term 'Communicative Competence' refers to a broader notion of language proficiency that encompasses listening, speaking, reading and writing, plus appropriate skills for conversational and academic speech. Culturally relevant skills are listed under the sections Socio-linguistic and Strategic Competencies on the opposite page. This graphic illustrates the interdependence of skills that are necessary for Communicative Competence in English.

Many English-speaking individuals, who work for multinational corporations, have good literacy skills and are competent speakers of English. The most common areas of difficulty expressed are cross-cultural miscommunications, pronunciation, a narrow range of English vocabulary and an insufficient knowledge of social conventions.

Policy-makers and educators of ELL must extend their understanding of what English proficiency entails and plan for the instruction of all the skills sets involved in Communicative Competence.

Knowing the Challenges

2. Challenges Specific to English

Specific English Challenges

1. Spoken and Written Language Differences

2. Syllables, Stress and Pronunciation

3. Word, Phrase and Sentence Intonation

4. Sentence and Discourse Complexities

5. Cultural Literacy and Assumptions

English Speaking Proficiency

Requires Student Competence in these Four Areas

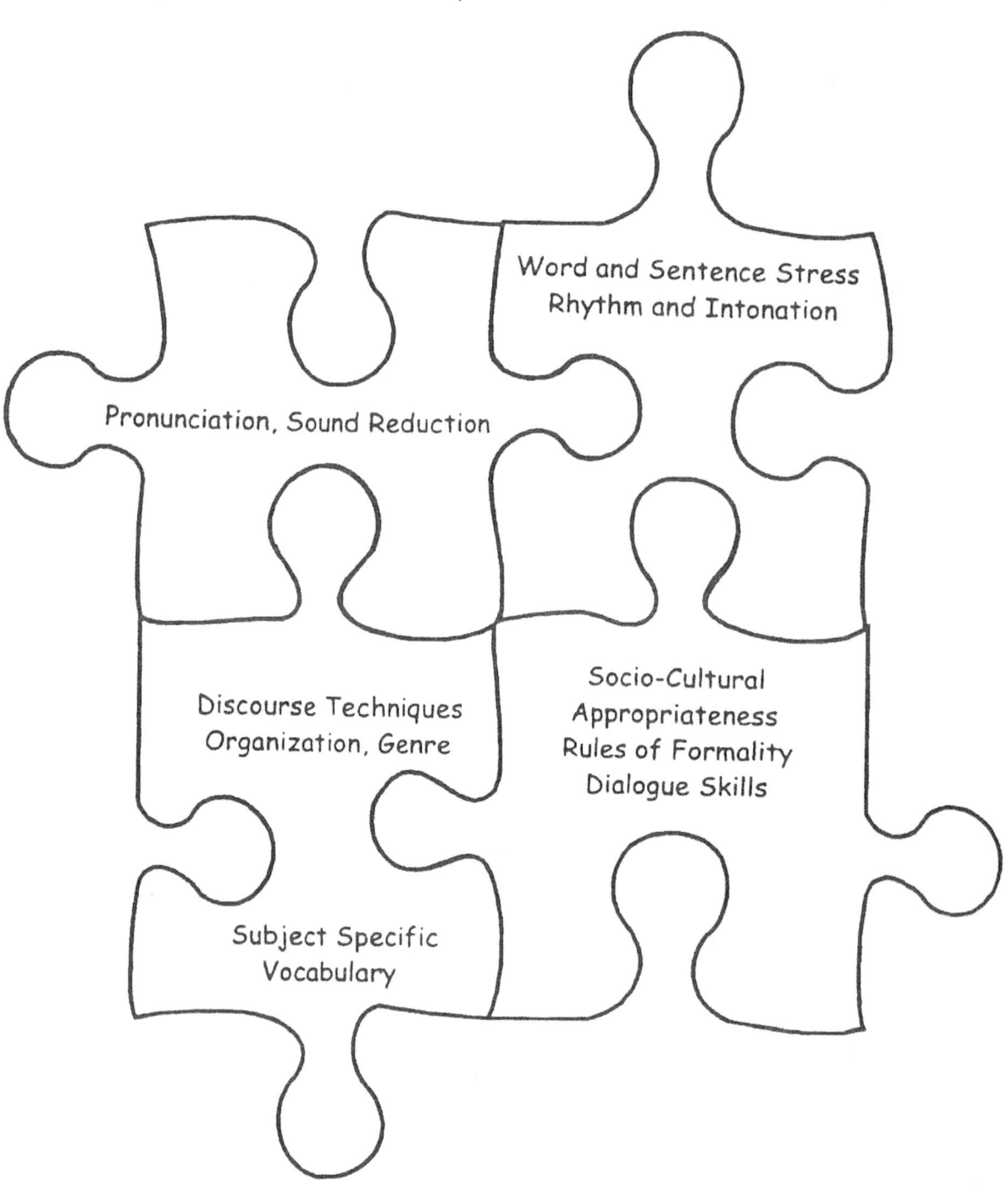

What is the Difference Between Speaking and Writing English?
Word Blending, Omissions, and Sound Variations

A) The following examples demonstrate some of the main differences between spoken and written English. On the left are sentences printed phonetically. Figure out what they say? Next, read the sentences with Standard English writing. Identify the differences between spoken and written English.

1. Stan dup.	1. Stand up.
2. Wha zat?	2. What's that?
3. Cudja gimme a penso?	3. Could you give me a pencil?
4. Whahdeeya wan?	4. What do you want?
5. Wha zee doin?	5. What is he doing?
6. Wha tsa madr?	6. What is the matter?

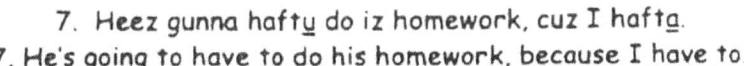

7. Heez gunna haft<u>u</u> do iz homework, cuz I haft<u>a</u>.
7. He's going to have to do his homework, because I have to.

B) Pronounce the following words. Notice the middle sound.
    letter   better   butter   water   settle

C) What is the final sound of these past tense verbs?
    dropped   shouted   spelled

D) Language learners often perceive English speaking as an "acoustic blur". They can't tell where one word ends, and the other begins. Speaking involves speed, intonation, word and phrase emphasis. How can teachers help comprehension?

Language Conscious Teaching
Articulation of Blended Sounds in English Speech

Language Learners are challenged specifically by the English articulation pattern of blending or linking the end sounds of one word with the beginning sound of the next. The following examples come from Judy Gilbert's text, <u>Clear Speech</u>, Cambridge University Press. As you work through the following examples, just imagine the befuddlement of your students. These speaking patterns might transfer into English spelling errors.

Blended Sounds with Vowels

1. A vowel sound at the end of a word blends with the vowel sound at the beginning of the next word.
   - coffee and milk - coffeean milk/cof feein milk
   - have an apple - havan napple

2. The "N" sound at the end of a word blends with another "N" or a vowel at the beginning of the next word.
   - Don is - don-nis
   - John knows - John-nnows
   - Joan always - Joan-nalways
   - An ice cube - anice cube

"M" blends with words that start with a vowel. "L" does too
   - Come on - cah mon
   - Turn the <u>alarm off</u> - alarm moff
   - a bowl of soup - a bola soup

Language Conscious Teaching
Articulation of Blended Sounds in English Speech

Here are other blending patterns.
Consonants t, d, p, k and the strong g (go)
at the end of a word blend with a following vowel.

Write the English spoken version for the following words.
bad apples - ba dapples
hold it - hol di
pick it up - pic kit dup
great idea -
paid it -
sit on -
had a -
spend all -
cook all -
keep all -
stop it -
Get out your book. -
bag of -

Write these as they would be spoken.
who are -
what did you -
would you -
teeth are -
something -

Howdee ya help studenz move from the English pronunciation
nin speech tuh spelling in literacy?

33

Language Conscious Teaching
Articulation of Noun-Verb Words in English

Pronounce these words first as a noun and then as a verb. Finally, mark English word stress and note any patterns.

Nouns	Verbs
conflict	conflict
survey	survey
record	record
structure	structure
support	support
model	model
program	program
list	list
plot	plot
drive	drive
base	base

What are the adjective forms, if any, for the words above?

Language Conscious Teaching
Articulation of Verb and Related Noun Formations in English

Write the noun formed from each verb.
Pronounce these words as a verb and then as a noun.
Finally, mark English word stress and note any patterns.

Verbs	Nouns
encourage	
arrange	
describe	
occur	
notice	
repeat	
inform	
solve	
evolve	
create	

Suffix

Read these verbs and their nouns. Say a sentence for the nouns.

describe	descrip<u>tion</u>
identify	identification
multiply	multiplication
add	addition
subtract	subtraction
invent	invention
pollute	pollution
imagine	imagination
celebrate	celebration
destroy	destruction
inform	information
decorate	decoration
introduce	introduction
graduate	graduation

Language Conscious Teaching
English Word Stress, Syllable Stress in Words with a Suffix

Mark syllable stress in these words and note any patterns.

Root Word	Suffix
	-ity
possible	possibility
able	ability
active	activity
mature	maturity
responsible	responsibility
diverse	diversity
	-ic
magnet	magnetic
drama	
athlete	
apology	
alcohol	
economy	
	-ical
alphabet	alphabetical
history	
theory	
politics	
chemistry	
electric	

The previous task was meant to illustrate the complexity of English pronunciation. Do not teach this stress rule directly.

Sentence Stress

Audio-lingual Methods in the Curriculum

In Audio-lingual methodology, students hear a word or a short phrase, and repeat it back to the teacher. 'Acoustic blur' happens when students can't make out where one word ends and the other begins, so the audio-lingual method makes students much more comfortable while learning new vocabulary. This method is very teacher-directed. Pictures can assist comprehension and peers (or bi-lingual dictionaries) help when concepts need translation.

Audio-lingual lessons allow a teacher to reinforce proper pronunciation and give students feedback right away. This method is used for newcomers to English, for new spelling lists in junior grades, and even in high schools for multi-syllabic words.

After practice with short, predictable speech patterns that guide language use, ELLs can move on to Shared Reading, which is similar to Choral Reading in that every student speaks at the same time. Teachers can help ELLs and Special Needs students to read longer sentences and paragraphs using shared reading. Photocopy an important section of text or story. Make sure the text is larger than in a textbook. Partner Reading is also a useful technique when information is taught from a textbook.

In junior grades and up, any informational material with complex sentences and lengthy discourse should raise a 'red flag' for teachers of ELLs. ELLs will lose sight of the main sentence if it is embedded with phrases and clauses. The problem is so easy to notice if teachers ask an ELL to read this type of discourse. The intonation alone will appear stilted and strange as ELLs look for meaning and become confused with the sentence construction.

English Speech
Sentence Stress in English

English speakers stress nouns, verbs, adverbs, adjectives and question words in sentences, but usually do not put any stress on pronouns, prepositions, conjunctions or helping verbs (modals).

Intonation refers to vocal pitch. In English, we use intonation to convey emotions, highlight important information and much more. "You did that?" "It's a beautiful day, isn't it?" ". . at nine o'clock."

Intonation changes in phrases and clauses within a sentence. Even pauses add meaning or assist with clarity of a message. We use rising and falling intonation patterns to create the rhythms of English. Some Asian languages use pitch to create a different meaning. In Mandarin, 'na' spoken with a rising pitch means to take, but spoken with a falling pitch, 'na' means to pay taxes.

Don't attempt to teach such linguistic features to Elementary students. In order to increase your ELLs' proficiency with spoken English, become a model of informal language in discussions, conversations, questioning, rhymes and jokes. Model more formal and academic speech through reading, drama or multi-media.

Another very useful and direct approach to helping ELLs with intonation in lengthy sentences or using content discourse is to write out several important sentences relevant to the content, and have students look while you read the section with emphatic intonation. Read again but have students repeat the intonation of each section after you. Next, guide students in dividing the speech segments with a slash at pauses, and marking the rising and falling patterns with line strokes. After you read a final time, ask students to try reading the piece with proper intonation.

Language Conscious Teaching
Sentence Stress in English

Practise marking phrase and meaning pauses with a slash, and indicate rising and falling intonation with lines above the text.

Example

Daniel / thought about his mother, his father and his brother, Sam. /

Would they come to Canada?

Marker, Medical Suspense, Robin Cook, Thorndike Press, 2005

"In the wee hours of February 2, a cold, steady drizzle drenched the concrete spires of New York City, shrouding them in a dense swirl of purplish-pink fog. Save for a few muted sirens, the city that never sleeps was at a relative standstill. Yet at exactly three-seventeen a.m., two nearly simultaneous, unrelated but basically similar, microcosmic events occurred on opposite sides of Central Park that would prove to be fatefully connected. One was on a cellular level, the other on a molecular level."

Stress, Pauses and Intonation with Content

Choose a paragraph, text section or a summary, and print it on the following form or on a computer using size 16 and double line spacing. Also, copy the work onto an overhead transparency.

1. Hand out a copy of the work and inform students that they will practise marking stress, pauses and English intonation.
   First, have students read the passage to themselves.
   Then the teacher reads the passage aloud at a slightly less than normal speed.

2. Turn on the overhead projector so all students can work along.
   Ask students to listen again and identify 'words' that are stressed.
   (word stress not syllable stress)
   Use an upward slash across the top of the word to mark stress.
   Mark these on the transparency text.
   Have students mark the stressed words on their own copies.

3. Next, ask students to listen for pauses (i.e., often after stressed words, connecting words, phrases, even adjectives).
   Mark pauses with downward slashes at the end of the word.
   Do this on the transparency and students work on their copies.

4. Then, the teacher reads and marks rising and falling intonation for each sentence.

5. When this is complete, the teacher reads the whole text again exemplifying all of the stresses, pauses and intonation.

6. Finally, have students read the passage to a partner.

Note
Foreign students who use a handheld, voiced, bilingual dictionary will already be familiar with marks for syllabication, word stress and intonation.

Sentence Stress and Intonation

Topic _____   Student _____

Discourse
Language Complexities in Lengthy Spoken or Written English

Language Conscious Teaching
Competence with English Discourse

Proficient English speakers understand the lengthy, complex discourse of texts, speeches or university lectures. They understand how to access content from different genre.

1. Read through the following passage about Discourse.
2. Highlight only the main sentences in the paragraphs.

Language as Discourse and Language in Discourse
It seems necessary to attempt a reformulation or at least a re-positioning of the discursive context for the language teacher in higher education, whether an academic literacy specialist, or intercultural academic literacy specialist, i.e. EAP teacher. Furthermore, although the 'I'm just a language teacher' position might be held in some quarters, that concept of 'language' might not be quite so emaciated as the formulation suggests. Language teachers in higher education are likely to be highly qualified and aware of the complexities of uses and functionings of language.

Academic literacy practices vary across cultures, as do interactional styles between tutor and student. Bloor and Bloor for example warn against 'the false expectation that educational structures and systems do not differ internationally. Students, unless they have been instructed to the contrary, may believe that universities in Britain operate very similarly to those in their own country.'(Bloor & Bloor, 1991, p2 in Adams et al). Differences in interactional styles between tutors and students, differences in expectations of how understanding is shown, and differences in the degree to which something is taught and something is researched all play a role in the context of L2 speakers of English studying in an English speaking country. This is an awareness which EAP practitioners have, as they expend a great deal of energy in finding out what the underlying educational value systems of their students are in order to facilitate their understanding of and transition to a different academic culture.

Paper presentation, English Language Conference on Education, University of Hong Kong

Discussion Topics

1. What difficulties did you experience with this text?

2. How did you express your frustrations?

3. How could discourse issues affect your ELLs?

Language Conscious Teaching
Language Learners as Writers

Writing, Year 1 - Year 2
Students supported in task which is immediately relevant, and connected to speech

1. Learns print and/or cursive letter forms with help
2. Copies words, phrases or simple sentences
3. Language Experience, students copy teacher's chart
4. Types work on a computer. Attends to punctuation
5. Composes repeated or patterned sentences
5. Composes short personal pieces on his/her own
6. Uses high frequency vocabulary. Begins to spell

Writing, Year 2 - Year 4
Students supported with feedback, peer translation, relevant context

1. Facility with print and cursive styles, punctuation
2. Composes a page or more of narrative event
3. Growing use of conjunctions and cohesive devices
4. Writes longer pieces but not complex sentences
5. Understands and uses paragraphs and details
6. Able to edit with ease when taught the process
7. Makes huge leap in use of literate-type vocabulary
8. Able to follow, and may name, writing genre
9. Begins to use word attack skills in spelling

Discourse - Talk and Write

Answer these questions.
Say the answers.
Write the answers.
Print all the answers on a computer - like a story.
Read your story to a partner.
Read your story to the class.

1. What movie did you see? I saw _____

2. Where did you see the movie? I watched it _____

3. What is the movie about? The movie is about _____

4. Who is in the movie? _____

5. Why do you like that movie? It is a good movie because ___

6. What is the name of another good movie? Another good __

Cultural Dissonance Affects Learning

Dissonance refers to a lack of agreement in beliefs, and when educators refer to 'cultural dissonance' this concept of 'different beliefs' enlarges greatly. In education, cultural dissonance can include topics such as individual worldviews, cultural anthropology, a variety of fields of psychology such as behavioural, pathology, and learning. Educators readily recognize differences in language, clothing, food, religion and customs (actions based on cultural traditions or religious beliefs).

There are, however, many other ramifications from cultural dissonance, not the least of which is an implicit assumption that students share the same 'common knowledge' when presented with North American stories, novels and other forms of literacy. Cultural Literacy refers to this form of dissonance in which ELLs either do not possess a common, shared knowledge assumed by an author, or the information runs contrary to a student's own cultural norms.

Language learners come from backgrounds over which they had no control and they enter the learning environment of our schools, over which they have no control.

Cultural Literacy

To be culturally literate, students must be cognizant of the shared, common knowledge of implicit and explicit traditions, values and literary conventions in the stories, novels and other art forms of the host culture.

In class, ELLs may lack prior knowledge of information or nuance in both speech and literary text that could assist meaning.

Before presenting a piece of text, teachers should

- preview the lecture, speech or text for cultural content
- initiate discussion about the cultural reference(s)
- elicit prior knowledge of a concept
- identify idiomatic expressions

What is Your Function?

English Language Functions

What is a language function?
Function refers to a **specific purpose** for using language.

Here is an example:
You want something, you ask for it, say please and thank you.

Language Function - asking or requesting
Related Language Skills - Forming questions, "?" punctuation
Related Vocabulary - Please, Thank you, Could I, May I
Related Socio-Cultural Knowledge - formal/informal, slang

In the example above, when you want something, you must know how to structure a question in English. You have to know to put the question mark in writing.

You have to use culturally appropriate forms of politeness, and the appropriate use of formal or informal language.

You must know the correct pronunciation, word and syllable stress and intonation when you are asking a question.

Language Proficiency requires that students know English functions with related vocabulary, related literacy, and the appropriate social and cultural norms.

What is a Language Function?
Cohesive Devices as Functions

Cohesive devices, sometimes called signal or connecting words, join phrases, clauses, and sentences to make ideas flow and to show the relationship of ideas. Basic conjunctions 'and', 'or' and 'but', are the simplest cohesive devices. Here are more.

Function	Related Vocabulary
1. to show sequence	first, second, etc
2. to show time relationships	then, after, finally, while
3. to compare	both, similarly, as well
4. to contrast	although, however, so
5. to list details	also, as well, in addition, moreover
6. to conclude	therefore, in conclusion, consequently

English Language learners will need to be taught how and when to use these functions and related words. This is especially imperative since we *expect students to use them in writing, group work and for oral presentations*. The following ideas use supported, shared speech and writing activities that teach students how to use the correct vocabulary as cohesive devices.

English: Functions of Communications

> A 'function' refers to the reason for communicating.
> Do your students know the words and tone of voice required for these:

___ Introductions - This is . . . , I want to introduce . . .
___ Politeness - proper words formal and informal
___ Asking - from a teacher or adult - Mr. Brown would like to . . .
___ Seeking permission - May I . . . please . . . , Is it alright if . . .
___ Expressing needs - I need . . ., Could you please . . ., May I . . .
___ Expressing Likes, Dislikes and Preferences . . .
___ Expressing Sympathy/Condolences/Congratulations - Please accept
___ Expressing Agreement - Oh yes, that's fine/a good idea, Sure, Okay
___ Expressing Disagreement - I don't agree with . . . No, I don't think
___ Giving Orders - imperative sentences
___ Giving Directions - for a place or a task sequence
___ Offering Assistance/Food/Get-togethers - May I . . Would you like
___ Expressing Opinions - I believe that . . . In my opinion . . . I think . . .
___ Making Suggestions - Wouldn't you . . ., I think you should . . . etc
___ Giving Advice - You ought to . . . I'd suggest that . . . My advice is . . .
___ Complaining - Excuse me but, This . . . . , I want to . . . .
___ Making a Comparison - this, and that, both, also, etc.
___ Contrasting - the same, different from, but, however, although
___ Sequencing - first, second, third, next, then, after that . . ., etc
___ Interviewing - forming and sequencing appropriate questions
___ Debating - Persuasion Techniques, Rebuttal Techniques
___ Delivering a Speech/Presentation
___ Knowledge of Genre Styles - drama, poetry, recipes, experiments

___
___
___

Summary - Summarize

Ensure that students translate or understand summary and summarize.
Start with oral work. Move from easy to more challenging summaries

1. What did you learn in school/Science/on TV today?

2. What rules do you need to follow at home?

3. Do you want a pet? Why or why not?

4. Tell me about a movie/comic/video that you saw/like.

5. Listen to this sentence. Tell me what you think and give me reasons and examples.
    a) I'm a lucky person.
    b) Some foods keep you healthy.
    c) Robots are useful inventions.

6. Do you know the story about _____?
   (Red Riding Hood/The Three Bears/_____)
   What was it about? (Elicit sequence and details.)

7. Listen to this word and explain to me what it's about.
    i.e., school, pollution, technology, music, government

8. Listen to this paragraph, then tell me what it's about.
    Your choice of an informational paragraph, not a sequence.

Summary of _____

Name _____

 # Writing a Recipe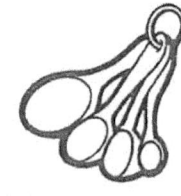

How to make _____

Temperature _____   Cooking/Baking Time _____

Ingredients:

_____   _____
_____   _____
_____   _____
_____   _____

Instructions:

1.

2.

3.

4.

5.

6.

7.

Continue on reverse side...

How to Compare Things

Compare means to tell about what is the same
and also what is different about two or more things.

1. A Park and A Beach
What's the same?
A park and a beach are both great places to go and have fun, **and** you can have a picnic in either place. The park might have a playground and a walking path, although many beaches do too.

What's the difference?
Obviously, you can swim at the beach but not at the park. You will need a towel and a swim suit for the beach, but you wear just normal clothes for the park. Usually, a park is closer to your house, but you will definitely need a car to get to a beach.

2. A Hamburger and a Pizza
What's the same?_____

_____

What's the difference? _____

_____

3. Fresh Water and Salt Water
What's the same?_____

_____

What's the difference?

_____

A Compare and Contrast Game

* Student groups of 3 or 4 brainstorm as many likenesses or differences as possible as they are on a time limit. One person writes down the group answers. The group with the most correct answers wins that round and gets a point. The group that has the most points wins the game. Every tie gets a point.

*Groups ought to have anywhere from 1-3 minutes to list their answers, which will be shared with the whole class.

1. Differences between a campfire/fire and a BBQ.

2. Similarities between a lake and a river.
   (freshwater, drinkable, can fish, swim, boat, etc.)

3. Differences between a polar bear and a panda bear.

4. Similarities between a wolf and a dog.

5. Differences between a house and an apartment.

6. Similarities between using a snorkel and mask and SCUBA.
   (SCUBA = Self-contained underwater breathing apparatus)

Compare Summer Words

hotel and a motel

a snorkel and SCUBA

a lake and a river

a beach and a pool

a tent and a trailer

a park and a beach

a suntan and a sunburn

a holiday and a camp

Writing Know How

Use the following vocabulary and activities as an oral introduction before written work.

1. Compare means how things seem the same.

both   the same...   just like   also   as well

alike   They are equally...   They are similar because...

2. Students volunteer ideas to compare –
    2 Fast Food Places
    a Beach and a Park

---

3. **Contrast** means how things are different.

but   however   different   unlike

instead   on the other hand   in contrast

although   even though   nevertheless

4. Students volunteer ideas to contrast –

    Vegetables or Pizza
    Dogs and Cats

How to Contrast Two Things

Contrast means to tell only the difference between things.

1. A Movie Theater and a Video

You have to go to a movie theater **but** you can watch videos at home. You can watch a movie on a huge screen **and also** the sound is better than on a video. **However**, movies cost a lot more money.

2. A Can of Pop and a Glass of Juice

_____

_____

_____

3. Wild Animals and Tame Animals

_____

_____

_____

4. A reason and an excuse

_____

_____

_____

Assignment – Cut and paste 2 large pictures on a piece of construction paper, and then write a paragraph contrasting the two. Use the appropriate vocabulary.

Compare & Contrast = Same & Different

1. Model a "compare and contrast" task by working through examples as a class.

2. Fill in the graphic organizer first through discussion, and then model the way a comparison paragraph could be made. Focus on the word 'both'. Finally, develop sentences to show contrast using "but", "however" and "although". Then, show the use of a Venn Diagram for speed.

3. Use "compare" and 'contrast' organizers for novel studies, science, history, etc.

Express Your Opinion
How to say what you think or believe

1. Read these sentence starters that show you how to state an opinion.

a) <u>I think that</u> homework is a good idea.
b) <u>I believe that</u> homework is a good idea because . . . .
c) <u>In my opinion,</u> homework is not a good idea because . . . .
d) <u>It is my opinion that</u> kids need time for sports and play, and that. . .
e) <u>My opinion is that</u> parents and kids need to spend more time . . . . .

2. Think about your opinion of these things. Do this yourself..
    reading   pollution   cooking   technology

3. Now, express your opinions about those things with a partner.

4. What is a topic that interests you? Write it on the line below. Write a paragraph to state your opinion about the topic and also to explain why you think that way.

5, Use the back of this paper.

What's Your Topic _____

Your Name _____

State Your Opinion

_____
Topic

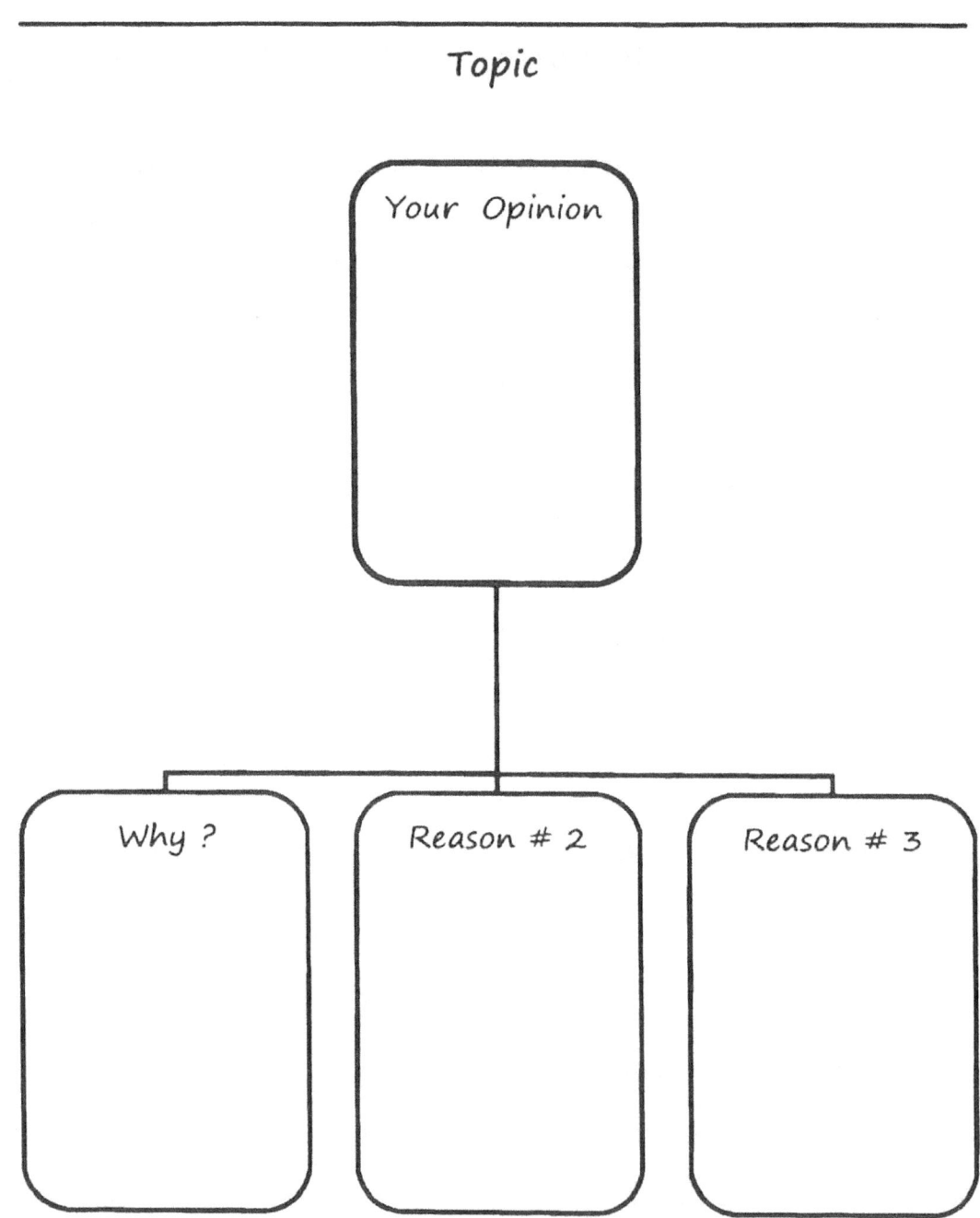

Now, express your opinion and write a paragraph on the reverse side.

Cause and Effect

The best way to teach cause and effect is to guide students through a topic relating to current studies or topics such as the environment, a book or novel, or school rules, etc.

'Motive' is implicit in the concept of cause and effect, and in the events and actions in books, movies, news, and life in general. The term 'motive' must be introduced and explained as the reason why something happens. The word 'motive' should be used often in order to consolidate students' understanding.

In addition, 'motive' often relates to personality traits as the reasons for an effect. This means that students, especially English language learners, will require several lessons on words that describe personality. i.e., envy (envious), greed (greedy, greedily), self-serving, honest, nervous, sociable, loner, etc.

Writing Explanations

An explanation tells why something happened.
It tells the cause of something, the reasons.
Write the reasons or cause of the following events:

Two people were fighting.
_____
_____
_____

The lights went out and the power went off.
_____
_____
_____

Your mom was late.
_____
_____
_____

He failed a test.
_____
_____
_____

The trip was canceled.
_____
_____
_____

Writing about Cause and Effect

Cause is the reason why something happened, and effect is what happens after. When writing about cause and effect you need to explain both 'the why' and the results. Some of the results may be long-term.

1. Pollution
Causes – throw-away plastic things, chemicals dumped in the water, air pollution from factories
Effects – sickness and health problems, unsafe drinking water, damage to the environment

2. Passed a test
Causes _____
_____

Effects _____
_____

3. Bullying
Causes _____
_____

Effects _____
_____

Writing Know How

Use the following vocabulary and activities as an oral introduction before written work. Have students listen while you enunciate each word and provide a sentence. Ensure comprehension and translation if needed.

1. Explaining Cause and Effect

causes   because of   for that reason   as a result

since   and then   also   leads to   due to

has the effect of   consequently   therefore

and the problems continue   in the end   lastly

2. Students use a word and volunteer ideas for this topic –

- When the Electricity Goes Off

3. Lastly, students volunteer ideas for the following topic and copy the paragraph(s) as you write it on the board.

- Why Exercise is Necessary

Types of Writing

Expository Writing – Explains Ideas, Gives Information, Steps
　　　　　　　　　　Based on Logic, Reasoning, Facts, Details
　　　　　　　　　　Main Idea, Details and a Conclusion

Narrative Writing – Tells a Story, True or Creative or Personal
　　　　　　　　　　Has Characters and Settings
　　　　　　　　　　Sequenced - a Beginning, a Middle and an End

Persuasive Writing – States your Opinion and Gives Your Reasons
　　　　　　　　　　Influences Someone's Decision
　　　　　　　　　　Techniques include Facts, Imagery, Pros and
　　　　　　　　　　Cons, Value Statements, Personal Experience

Descriptive Writing – Develops a Readers' Response to Something
　　　　　　　　　　is a Word Picture using Senses and Imagery
　　　　　　　　　　Creates an emotion, an important impression
　　　　　　　　　　Bkgd: youtube.com/watch?v=ATysG32zrsE

Reference:
http://www.teach-nology.com/worksheets/language_arts/creative/

Grade-level Resources: www.teach-ology.com

Student Activities for Writing Styles

Expository Writing
- Students develop a list of rules for a topic ie school/home/tech use, bullies, racism
- write a 'how to' regarding an experiment, a computer situation, a skill. Etc.
- Students write a news article using the 5 Ws
- Students provide explanations for an event/choice/invention
- Students provide the logic behind a story decision/historical event/current news
- Essay writing

Narrative Writing
- Student journals
- Students write ideas about a topic the teacher puts on the board.
- Personal Feedback from students regarding a book/lesson/event/situation
- Using magazine pictures to create a story with characters, places, events
- Students write an alternate ending to a story
- Students share story writing taking turns where the last student left off.
- Students offer an opinion with reasons
- Students relate a timeline of events/a cause and effect

Persuasive Writing
- creatind a print ad
- creating an advertisement to videotape
- sharing opinions
- developing Pro-Con charts
- writing a Pro or Con piece
- evaluating an argument and responding
- Students creat an Aesop-type story o teach a value/moral lesson
- Essay writing

Descriptive Writing
- Lesson worksheets on 'how to' are included
- Students identify a descriptive text section/sentences and rewrite it using similar words from a thesaurus.
- Students describe themselves/a friend/a relative/the teacher/etc.
- Students develop a scenario on an emotion

Writing
Narrative Writing has a Beginning, a Middle and an End

The Beginning

The Middle

The End

Activities

Write about some interesting news in the boxes.

Write a short story in the boxes.

Writing about a Process

You have practiced this idea with your teacher;
now, write a process paragraph about one of these topics.

1. How to be a good friend
2. How to train a dog
3. How to do an experiment
4. Learning to cook
5. How to draw or ski or ...
6. Your idea...

Title_____

Step 1 – Introduction – It's good to know how to, It's fun to,
This paragraph will explain how to...

Step 2 – First, _____

Step 3 - After that, then, the next thing you have to do _____
Secondly, Thirdly, Next

Step 4 – Next, then, after that
It's also a good idea to _____
It's important to _____
I suggest that _____
Following that, _____

Step 5. The last thing, _____   Finally, _____

Conclusion: _____

Describing
Give 3 ideas that describe each topic.

Sight - Feelings - Sound - Touch - Smell - Taste

1. Puppy

-

-

-

2. Water

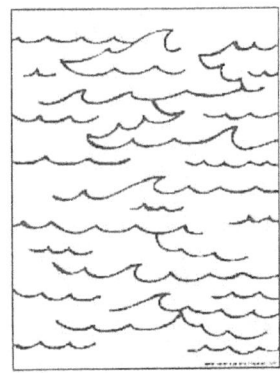

-

-

-

3. The City

-

-

-

Writing a Description
Assist students step-by-step. Students prepare their own examples for each. (alone/partners)

1. of a person or animal– appearance – attributes – actions

what they look like   personality   what they do

2. of a place – appearance, why you are there, emotion, history

what it looks like   how it makes you feel   where, why, uses

3. of a thing – size, what it's made from, how it feels, color, use

Brainstorm a Description

Item - _____

Mood, Emotion, Feeling

How it Looks – Sight and Location

What it's Doing and How it Moves

How it Feels - Touch

Listen – What Sounds

Any Smells - Scent

Writing a Description

You have practiced this idea with your teacher;
now, write a description and details about these topics.

1. Your favorite food

_____
_____
_____
_____
_____

2. Your favorite person

_____
_____
_____
_____
_____

3. Your favorite place

_____
_____
_____
_____
_____

Check your work. Did you
- tell about your feeling or emotion?
- use color, texture, taste, or actions?
- refer to previous experiences?
- compare or contrast it to something else?

Adjectives

> What is an Adjective?
> An adjective describes a noun.
> An adjective can tell;
> Color(s)
> Size
> Number
> Quality(s)

Examples

1. The <u>blue</u> ball rolled away.

2. The <u>big, blue</u> ball rolled away.

3. The <u>six, big, blue</u> balls rolled away.

4. The <u>six, big, beautiful, blue</u> balls rolled away.

5. The <u>six, big, beautiful, blue, plastic</u> balls rolled away.

Note
A comma separates two or more adjectives.

> An adjective describes a noun.
> An adjective can tell;
> size
> color
> number
> quality

Write size adjectives.

a _____ baby   the _____ candy   _____ hair

Write color adjectives.

a _____ car   a _____ toy   the _____ apple

Write number adjectives.

_____ helicopters   _____ taxis   _____ baot

Write qualities.

_____ story   _____ child

_____ chairs   _____ game

_____ food   _____ student

_____ coat   _____ artwork

_____ singer   _____ movie

> An adjective describes a noun.
> An adjective can tell;
> size
> number
> color
> quality

Write adjectives.

1. Your _____ brother is cool.
2. _____ , _____ monkeys laughed at me.
3. I have _____ , _____ jackets.
4. Do you want _____ bananas or _____ apple?
5. Look at the _____ , _____ baby.
6. My mother has a _____ , _____ car.
7. That _____ , _____ T.V. cost $7000.
8. I made a _____ , _____ mistake.
9. Mary walked across the _____ street.
10. Peter has _____ , _____ video games.
11. I wanted _____ , _____ sandwiches.
12. Let's order a _____ and _____ pizza.

_____ story   _____ movie

_____ friend   _____ dinner

Adjectives tell Quality

1. Some adjectives tell the quality of emotions and feelings.

sad	lonely	depressed	angry	miserable
happy	excited	bored	crazy	curious
silly	exciting	wonderful	horrible	stupid
fabulous	interesting	goofy	funny	cool
scary	terrible	terrific	humorous	shy

2. Some adjectives tell what something is made from.

plastic	wooden	homemade	cotton
gold	rubber	brick	cement
silk	glass	steel	Styrofoam

3. Some adjectives tell how a thing feels when you touch it.

| soft | warm | fuzzy | comfortable |
| hard | freezing | smooth | flat |

4. Write the opposite quality.

expensive _____   light _____

thin _____   sharp _____

best _____   square _____

low _____   positive _____

Believe Me When I Tell You

* Persuasive Writing is a form of Opinion Writing.

* It's easy to learn the concept by studying commercials.

I strongly suggest that teachers watch the following short videos. They're very good, succinct and clear, and will help you decide what and how to approach student instruction regarding persuasive writing samples and techniques.

1. https://www.youtube.com/watch?v=hD9arWXIddM

2. https://www.youtube.com/watch?v=yiexHnX0xZY2.

Recognizing Persuasive Techniques

Students will learn to recognize persuasive techniques in both writing and media and understand how they are used in order to affect other people's thinking and attitudes.

In Writing

These strategies are often used in writing to persuade:
1. making a value statement
2. using an expert's opinion
3. providing facts or data
4. appealing to logic
5. making a moral argument

In Commercials

These strategies are often used in advertisements to persuade:
1. a slogan and a logo
2. special effects and also music, color, movement and voice
3. using a celebrity, famous person, beautiful people, a rich lifestyle
4. offers a sale or discount
5. makes a value statement
6. uses humor
7. uses hyperbole
8. appeals to your emotion
9. uses words that affect choice (This is newer. That is _____)
10. uses repetition

Activities: Students will discuss the above information, also watch a commercial(s) and choose a print ad to identify the techniques and their validity.

Resource - Teacher's Guide and Student Activities Pages 7 and 8 from -
https://www.consumer.ftc.gov/Admongo/_pdf/curriculum/FTC-Lesson-Plans-Student-Worksheets.pdf
Reference - http://www.classzone.com/cz/books/ml_lit_gr12/resources/pdfs/media_analysis/HS_15_Ad_Techniques2.pdf

Different Points of View

A.

_____ thinks	_____ thinks
_____	_____
_____	_____
_____	_____
_____	_____

B.   *What I Think*

_____

_____

_____

_____

_____

_____

_____

The Problem

_____
_____
_____
_____

Solution #1
_____
_____
_____

Solution #2
_____
_____
_____

Solution #3
_____
_____
_____

Solution #4
_____
_____
_____
_____

- Which solution seems the best to you? Be prepared to say why you chose the solution you did.
- Put a red star ★ beside the solution you favour.

Persuasive Writing Format
Use Point Form

_____

Topic Sentence

Reason 1 plus an explanation or an example
_____
_____
_____
_____

Reason 2 plus an explanation or an example
_____
_____
_____
_____

Reason 3 plus an explanation or an example
_____
_____
_____
_____

Conclusion – State your original idea and use an interesting ending sentence
_____
_____
_____

Practice Composing an English Essay

Topic - Sports

Introduce your topic.
I think that soccer is the best sport in the world. In fact, Soccer is played all over the world. Every year there is a competition called the World Cup to see which country has the best team.

Now, you have to write 3 paragraphs
to tell different things about your topic

| Kids Soccer | Skills You Learn | Soccer Heroes |

Conclusion
Why is Soccer Your Favorite Sport?

Essay Format – Point Form Practice Sheet

Introduction – Grab attention, then state your topic and your opinion or claim.

Reason 1 – the most important one

Reason 2

Reason 3

Conclusion – Restate main idea and summarize proof

Practise an English Essay

Topic - _____

Introduction (3 sentences)
What will you write about? _____
Why is it interesting or important? _____
What are 3 things you'll talk about? _____

Use point form to make 3 paragraphs with different information.

_____ _____ _____
_____ _____ _____
_____ _____ _____
_____ _____ _____
_____ _____ _____
_____ _____ _____
_____ _____ _____
_____ _____ _____

Conclusion _____
_____
_____
_____

Instructions for Writing an Essay

Part 1 - Planning and Composing

Choose your topic and use the outline to guide your essay work.

a) Your topic sentence states the main idea you will be writing about.

b) Then write four to five sentences in each paragraph to explain each idea.

c) End the essay with a summary to support your introductory statement.

Part 2 - Read, Revise and Edit

Read your essay out loud and check that it makes sense. Fix it.

Make sure you used complete sentences.

Check that you used cohesive devices and compound sentences.

Use the Grammarly.com to check your grammar, spelling, and punctuation.

Use Thesaurus.com to find synonyms to improve your vocabulary use

Read your essay again.

Writing the Conclusion of an Essay
Your Last Paragraph

1st Sentence - Restate your main idea. (thesis)

2nd Sentence - Summarize the main idea of paragraph 2

3rd Sentence - Summarize the main idea of paragraph 3

4th Sentence - Summarize the main idea of paragraph 3

Last Sentence – Helpful Suggestions Below

One thing for sure is that ….   From now on …   We all realize that ….

There is sufficient evidence to conclude that …..   The end result is that …..

Without a doubt …..   It is important to understand that ….   It is clear that …..

What Comes First, Chicken or the Egg, Language or Literacy?

Associations of the Word

Generally speaking, a word has a clear and similar meaning for everyone.

The word 'cake' is easy to understand. It is a concrete object that is generally understood, even if our minds visualize different attributes: birthday cake, a wedding cake, a berry cake, a chocolate cake, an ice-cream cake, a bundt cake, a layer cake, a cheesecake.

However, native-English speakers also understand words that have multiple meanings whether they are found in slang or used in idiomatic speech. We have no trouble with 'cake' also meaning easy, as in 'piece of cake' or 'selling like hot cakes' or 'have your cake and eat it too' and that 'takes the cake', or 'cake it on' meaning apply something liberally. English language learners lack this range of vocabulary - although it's something we assume is common knowledge. ELLs do not have the same fluency, accuracy or range of vocabulary as native-English speakers.

Let's do another simple word - 'like'.

Generally understood meaning _____
Having similar attributes (simile) i.e., _____
Explain 'just like' _____

What is the function of like in the following sentences? _____
_____

So like, wow! As if like . . I had any idea! . . like um, wow, yeah, Amazing.

Language Conscious Teaching
Range of Vocabulary and Language Complexity - Semantics

What is the opposite of

bright ⟶

What are the different attributes of "bright"?
1.
2.
3.
4.

Write a context sentence for each attribute of "bright".
1.
2.
3.
4.

Research shows that English language learners do not have the **range or depth of vocabulary** as that of native English speakers.

Language Conscious Teaching
Literacy and Language Instruction

'How' Questions

1. How does literacy instruction account for words like 'bright' that have multiple attributes of meaning?

2. How does literacy instruction account for English Language Learners (ELLs) who don't know irregular past tense verbs?

3. How does literacy instruction account for ELL's who lack comprehension of task-based verbs in higher grades?
   i.e. skim, think critically, contrast, provide proof, jot down.

4. How do Literacy Initiatives address the problems of ELLs who lack competencies with complex sentence structures in textbooks, or who don't understand content-specific vocabulary requisite for the successful completion of grade curriculum and tests?

5. How do Literacy Initiatives account for 'Cultural Literacy'?

'Can' Questions

Can you separate English language learning and teaching from literacy?

Can literacy initiatives precede or supersede the language needs of ELLs?

Can Equity be assured for ELLs without an explicit focus on language?

Language and Literacy in the Curriculum

- Answers to all 'How' questions: It doesn't.

  Without explicit connections to language learning and instruction, literacy initiatives are incomplete and shortsighted.

- Answers to all 'Can' questions: No.

  There exists vast knowledge of 'best practices' for teaching and learning English in Elementary and Secondary schools. Literacy is a goal and a key aspect of any language training program. However, the most effective Literacy Initiatives arise from the need to improve language proficiencies for non-native speakers of English. The horse goes before the cart, so to speak.

  Language and Literacy instruction should look so interwoven in practice as to appear seamless. Fundamentally, Equity for ELLs cannot be assured without entwining Language and Literacy.

- Answer: Attributes of the word 'bright.'
  1. shine (opposite of 'dull.')
  2. intelligence
  3. personality (happy, cheerful)
  4. light intensity

Components of Academic Literacy

Academic Literacy ⟶
pivots on knowledge of vocabulary and semantics;
- comprehension of word meanings individually and in discourse
- word-attack skills which are decoding cues and include all phonetic capabilities, sound systems, word categories, word building (plurals, prefixes), word stress and syllabication
- proficiency with pronunciation and in spelling

Academic Literacy ⟶
requires expertise with the syntax, intonation and discourse styles of spoken and written English communication plus;
- knowledge of literary devices and techniques
- recognition of culturally embedded beliefs and values
- a high tolerance for ambiguity regarding certain texts

Academic Literacy ⟶
requires a high level of meta-cognitive skills;
- to deduce and to make meaning
- to advance learning and messaging in spoken and written English

Although Language precedes Literacy,
Literacy is always the goal.

Curriculum Speak: Developing English for Academic Literacy
Mary Meyers, Revised 2010, Mainstreams Publications Canada

Verbal interactions with native English speakers help us develop the fluency, accuracy and range of vocabulary that we need for academic success.

Verbs

Cognition and Constraints

Verb Comprehension, Cognition and Equity

There is a huge difference in the kinds of questions we ask students after the primary grades. By the time students reach grade 5, teacher expectations of student growth in maturation, logical thinking and cognitive abilities have changed and as a result the language used to elicit knowledge becomes more abstract and complex.

When teachers work on new curriculum topics, the 'what to do' or verb vocabulary could pose a major stumbling block for language learners in text questions, assignments, group talk, and tests.
The following 'what to do' verbs were taken from a grade 5 reader. Which verbs do you think your ELLs could read and pronounce correctly? Which verbs would your ELLs understand? What could you say to explain the meanings?

include	examine
apply	identify
infer	think critically
skim	predict
track	gather
jot down	state
assess	support
figure out	define
demonstrate	contrast
respond to	provide

Language Conscious Teaching

Task
Working With Verbs in the Classroom

One of the first things people notice in speech is an incorrect verb tense.

1. Try the past tense verb worksheet with all your students.
- Use it first as an individual assignment.
- Note who knows irregular past tense verbs.
- Do most students need to be taught this skill?

2. Use the Assignment Verbs Survey with several ELLs, and compare results with a native English speaker.
- Is this an area where students need help, to articulate meanings or give an explanation?

3. Note the steps involved in the Spelling activity. This is a typical approach to introducing new material to ELLs.

4. Use 'directed teaching' to work along with students on the 2-word verb phrases.

Past Tense Verbs
Irregular Verbs Pre-test

Student_____   Date_____

Write the past tense beside each verb.

send _____   sleep _____
spend _____   drive _____
lend _____   drink _____
bend _____   bite _____
grow _____   put _____
know _____   hit _____
shut _____   slide _____
take _____   hide _____
tell _____   bring _____
draw _____   fight _____
blow _____   think _____
throw _____   buy _____
meet _____   catch _____
feel _____   teach _____
find _____   fall _____
stand _____   tear _____
hold _____   wear _____
freeze _____ give _____
wake _____   shoot _____
speak _____   made _____
win _____   see _____
ride _____   eat _____
sit _____   read _____

Past Tense

1. Work with a partner to write the past tense of each verb.
2. Check your spelling with the teacher.

sleep	send
drive	spend
drink	lend
bite	bend
put	grow
hit	know
shut	slide
bring	fly
fight	draw
think	blow
buy	throw
catch	meet
teach	feel
fall	find
tear	stand
wear	sting
give	make
shoot	hold
win	freeze
ride	wake
eat	tell

Assignment Verbs Survey

✓ Can your ELL say the verb?
✓ Can your ELL explain the verb? (add context as required)

discuss	include
summarize	invent
list	imagine
explain	affect
examine	record (v)
provide proof	respond to
sequence events	prepare for
define	pick out
demonstrate	jot down
state	figure out
apply	note (v)
provide details	outline (v)
gather information	track (v)
identify	design (v)
infer	support (v)
predict	choose
compare	contrast
highlight	think critically
assess	observe
scan	skim
describe personality	

Student Name _____

Length of Time in Canada _____

Assignment verbs are from a Grade 5 Reader.

Verbs as Idiomatic Expressions

Please Look Out!

A) What do these verbs mean? Talk about it with a partner.
Talk about it with the teacher, and write a sentence as an example.

1. look after _____

2. look at _____

3. look out _____

4. look out for _____

5. look up _____

6. look into _____

7. look down on _____

8. look over _____

B) Match the correct verb above to the meaning below.

1. review the information _____

2. be careful _____

3. find in the dictionary _____

4. watch the baby _____

5. see out the window _____

6. investigate _____

Two Word Verb Expressions
Comprehension of Idiomatic Two-Word Verbs

Listen - Listen to the teacher read and explain the examples below.
Speak - Give examples of other sentences using the same verb.
Write - Write a sentence of your own.

act up - The little kid acts up all the time.
_____

cover up - The guy had to cover up his theft.
_____

bring up - The doctor said he would probably bring up.
_____

bring up - I want bring up that idea during our discussion?
_____

dream up - How did she dream up that idea?
_____

use up - If you use up all the ketchup, let me know.
_____

give up - Daniel had to give up music.
_____

fix up - Fix up this mess right now.
_____

fix up - She should fix up her work.
_____

take up - My brother is going to take up golf this summer.
_____

Two Word Verb Expressions
Comprehension of Idiomatic Two-Word Verbs

Listen - Listen to the teacher read and explain the examples below.
Speak - Give examples of other sentences using the same verb.
Write - Write a sentence of your own.

lay off - I told him to lay off bugging that little kid.
_____

lay off - The company has to lay off sixteen people.
_____

show off - He always shows off.
_____

let off - The judge let him off with a warning this time.
_____

keep off - Keep your feet off the table.
_____

made off with - The thief made off with the TV, DVD player and computer.
_____

take off - Take off out of here before they come.
_____

sign off - Okay everybody, sign off your computer and go.
_____

get off - I have to get off the subway at the next station.
_____

cut off - My parents cut me off from any T.V. when I failed the test.
_____

Gerunds

A Gerund is a noun-verb with <u>-ing</u>.

Example - reading, sleeping, helping, speaking, cooking, studying

- These sentences begin with a gerund. Finish these sentences.

    1. Playing tennis is _____.

    2. Reading is _____.

    3. Speaking English is _____.

    4. Spelling is _____.

    5. Dancing is

- Finish these sentences with a gerund.

    1. I like _____.

    2. My mother began _____ the cookbook.

    3. He started _____ for his test last night.

    4. We have finished _____.

    5. Don't keep _____ that.

    6. My sister enjoys _____ the piano.

    7. I don't like _____ those vegetables.

    8. I hate _____.

    9. Stop _____ so much.

    10. Do you remember _____?

Infinitives

Infinitives are verbs with 'to' in front. They are not the main verb.
Example - to run, to play, to catch, to fly

A. Write an Infinitive verb in these sentences.

1. I like _____ baseball.

2. He wants _____ with you.

3. I forgot _____ the milk.

4. We would like _____ the museum.

5. I decided not _____ to school today.

B. Finish these sentences with an Infinitive.

1. I am waiting _____.

2. John tried _____.

3. They intended _____.

4. Mary hoped _____.

5. The judge ordered her _____.

6. My mom allowed me _____.

7. I'd love _____.

8. My boss advised me _____.

9. His father asked him _____.

10. I promise _____.

Curriculum Speak
Target Language Skill - Conditionals, Inference and Prediction

Helping Verbs 'could, would and might' usually mean a possibility. These words are necessary for ELLs to know when they answer 'prediction and inference' questions.

Examples
1. I forget, but I think our test might be on Friday.
2. I could go if my mom lets me. That would be great.
3. It would be foolish to drink that filthy water.
4. He could be lost. I'm not sure, but he might be.

Primary Grade Activities

1. Each student gets a copy of the same sheet of paper with a squiggle on it. Students use the squiggle as the basis for a picture of their own creation. Finally, students complete this sentence under their picture.
   It could be a _____.

2. Start a similar activity using a circle, rectangle, etc. as the basis of a picture, but this time hold it up and ask students what it **might be**. Have students practice using the new sentence pattern - **It might be a __ .**

Junior and Senior Grade Activities

1. Use examples from a unit of study to **practise** 'prediction and inference' questions and answers using of 'helping verbs'.

Verbs - Future Tense Forms

There are several ways to indicate the future tense in English.

1. "Will" plus verb - indicates a promise or strong determination.
   For example - I **will pass** the test.
           He **will buy** a car.
           I **won't cut** my hair.   I **will not** = I **won't**

2. "Is/am/are going to" plus verb - shows an intention or plan.
   For example - She **is going to visit** the doctor after school.
           I **am going to watch** T.V. now.
           They **are going to play** soccer.

3. "Might" plus verb - means a future possibility
   For example - I **might go** to Canada.
           We **might play** basketball tonight.
           She **might help** you.

4. "Would" or "could" plus verb - shows a conditional action
   For example - I **would go** with you if I have enough time.
           They **would buy** a house if they won a lottery.
           He **could watch** T.V. if he finishes homework.
           It **could rain** this afternoon.

5. "Might be" or "could be" - a present or future possibility
   For example - This **might be** a mistake.
           They **might be** lost.
           He **might be** in love with you.
           It **could be** a scary movie.

English Verb Tenses

Present Tenses

1. Simple Present - He <u>watches</u> sports on TV.
2. Present Continuous - He <u>is watching</u> sports on TV.
3. Present Perfect - He <u>has watched</u> sports on TV every night.
4. Present Perfect Continuous - He <u>has been watching</u> sports on TV all day.

> Note:
> Continuous tenses always use the basic verb plus - ing.
> Perfect tenses always use have or had.

Past Tenses

1. Simple Past - He <u>watched</u> sports on TV.
2. Past Continuous - He <u>was watching</u> sports on TV.
3. Past Perfect - He <u>had watched</u> sports on TV instead of playing the sport.
4. Present Perfect Continuous - He <u>had been watching</u> sports on TV when it broke.

Future Tenses

1. Simple Future - He <u>will watch</u> sports on TV. (indicating an intention or promise)
   - He <u>is going to watch</u> TV. (indicates a plan or inevitability)
2. Future Continuous - He will be watching sports on TV.
3. Future Perfect - He <u>will have watched</u> sports on TV every night.
   - (This tense refers to the past.)
4. Future Perfect Continuous - He <u>will have been watching</u> sports on TV.

> Conditionals - could, would, should - I <u>would watch</u> TV if sports were on.
> Modals - helping verbs such as can, may, might, ought to, etc.

Don't say, "Said."

A) There are many verbs that express feelings or moods.
B) Read these words and translate any word you don't understand.
C) Think of sentences for each of these verbs with a partner.
D) Then, join another partnership and take turns reading your sentences.

1. asked _____
2. replied _____
3. screamed _____
4. whispered _____
5. told _____
6. gasped _____
7. warned _____
8. announced _____
9. argued _____
10. yelled _____
11. shouted _____
12. offered _____
13. pleaded _____
14. explained _____
15. cried _____
16. grumbled _____
17. mumbled _____
18. suggested _____
19. described _____

Assignment - In a group, create a skit using these verbs. One character could be a storyteller, a narrator, a witness or a News announcer.

Emotions are Feelings

In stories and in movies,
the events happen because of
someone's feelings or emotions.

Go to this Internet website and make your own list of words that describe emotions. List some emotion words and translate them.

www.english-at-home.com
/vocabulary/english-word-for-emotions

_____

_____

_____

Knowing the Challenges

3. Identifying a Language Skill

Curriculum Problem Areas

> Problem Skills for ELL Language and Academic Literacy

The linguistic items on the following pages usually require direct instruction, review, or the use of scaffolding strategies to ensure ELLs progress along the language skills continuum. The linguistic items are categorized under four distinct and yet overlapping components. Note that these lists might not cover every problem skill. However, this information is extremely useful for teachers:
- to identify the kind of language error a student makes
- to pinpoint an exact skill that needs work

In point of fact, the listed items may need to be practised in each new content unit until ELLs can manage a particular skill on their own.

Moreover, these lists are especially helpful for teachers to locate a language skill(s) that can be taught through a content unit.

This list is specific, and it's very useful for just that reason. Most often, language lists or rubrics are too general and have broad statements that really don't articulate specific language skills within the subset. Here are some ways to use the lists.

- Use the list to identify errors that your students make
- Highlight language use as students work through a text
- Acknowledge areas of difficulty to lessen anxiety

What! More Lists!

> To cross that 'Language Chasm'
> ELLs require skills in the areas of Word Attack, Sentence know-how, Grammar, Discourse, Subject-specific skills, culturally appropriate use of English, Genre and Functions.

The following pages identify language skills in those areas.

Educators don't need to memorize the following list(s).
Educators do need to view them as part of a language continuum.

Educators don't need to teach all the items on the lists.
Educators do need to identify those skills a student(s) is lacking.

Educators don't need to do extra work to practise language skills.
Educators do need to use 'language in content' activities.

Educators don't need to use every scaffold activity suggested.
Educators do need to incorporate language activities as needed.

Educators don't need to implement this information immediately.
Educators do need to start processing and internalizing this.

Educators don't need to put aside their prior training.
Educators do need to recognize that language is the basis of communication, of content. The better a student can express knowledge in English, the more equitable assessments will be.

Vocabulary Difficulties that Challenge ELL

- words with several meanings
- multi-syllabic words and long words never encountered
- unknown vocabulary
- verb tenses (irregular past, perfect, two-word verbs)
- culturally specific, cultural dissonance
- word sound (ch in Chris, chef, chocolate)
- word and syllable stress
- pronunciation of new vocabulary, names, places
- only one context known for a word used in a different way
- word becomes unfamiliar with addition of a prefix or suffix
- non-count nouns (no 's', fish, fog, homework, music)
- no knowledge of the correct use of formal vocabulary
- no knowledge of idioms, puns
- no word knowledge of subject specific terms
- 'concept' vocabulary versus concrete nouns
- word use in prepositional time phrases (on, at, in, since)
- noun to verb forms and visa versa (record, record)
- lack descriptive adjectives and evocative words
- other

Grammar Difficulties that Challenge ELL
A Linguistic Skills Subset

- loses comprehension in reading/listening to complex syntax
- unaware of English grammatical system and components
- punctuation errors beyond periods and question marks
- third person singular verb errors, noun-verb agreement
- how to answer by repeating part of the question

    How would the outcome have changed if Pat had not lost his wallet?
    If Pat had not lost his wallet . . . .

- sentences constructed only one way, lacks creative forms
- unknown language use (simile, metaphor, language functions)
- no knowledge or use of adjective phrases
- no knowledge or use of adverb phrases
- no knowledge or use of verb phrases
- no knowledge or use of clauses (dependent, independent)
- no knowledge or use of comparative structure or style
- no knowledge or use of complex sentence formations
- no knowledge or use of formal, academic expression
- unable to use complex language in text in their own writing
- doesn't know use of indirect speech (She said that . . .)
- run-on sentences or overuse of simple sentences
- knowledge and proper use of cohesive devices

Discourse Difficulties that Challenge ELL

- paragraphing, formation of a topic sentence
- loses comprehension during complex discourse
- loses comprehension during extensive verbiage
- problems with paraphrasing, summarizing, quoting
- unable to learn from text with multiple and varied clauses
- doesn't understand extensive use of descriptive vocabulary
- lacks knowledge of transition words, cohesive devices
- cannot locate main subject or verb in complex sentences
- scared by inabilities to cope with text-style English
- use of dictionaries inappropriate and time-consuming
- loses place reading dense text, as in many novels
- unfamiliar with cultural and religious references
- abbreviations unknown
- slang in dialogues disrupts comprehension
- unfamiliar with intonation and pausing of sentence parts
- becomes a word-by-word-reader, loses fluency
- takes much longer to discern information and detail
- not familiar with formal language used in speeches, debates
- requires practice to develop comfort with intonation

Subject-Specific Content Challenges for ELL
A Linguistic Skills Subset

- unknown words of all kinds, decoding doesn't help
- unable to access meaning from subject-specific text
- unfamiliar with discourse style used for instruction
- requires guidance forming subject style questions
- requires assistance with pronunciation
- requires assistance with intonation
- record-keeping, note-taking, point form
- text features require instruction
- unfamiliar with written requirements, procedures
- abstract, conceptual vocabulary requires translation
- homework difficulties
- dictionaries more problematic than helpful
- speed of instructions and general information sharing
- requires more modelling of required tasks/procedures
- different discourse styles used to prove, explain, debate
- reference notation
- doesn't understand responses to plagiarism
- doesn't understand how to avoid plagiarism
- other

Word-Attack Skills

1. How do phonics and word-attack skills differ?

Phonics refers to a sound system for a language. Word-attack skills refer to different ways that people can use to help figure out or decode words.

2. What are the word-attack skills?

   ✓ sounding out (phonics)

   ✓ rhyming

   ✓ looking at smaller parts inside a word

   ✓ identifying root words

   ✓ understanding prefixes and suffixes, endings

   ✓ knowledge of word types (compound words, rhyme segments, sound exceptions, i.e., fought, caught)

   ✓ Syllabication

3. What are other word decoding strategies?
   Reading skills such as prediction, context or pattern

Phonics:
A Subset of Word-Attack Skills

Phonics is one of a variety of 'word-attack skills' - preliminary literacy techniques that assist students with word recognition, pronunciation, reading, writing and language comprehension.

Phonics refers to sound-letter correspondence and includes knowledge of initial and final consonants, vowel sounds, consonant blends, medial sounds, digraphs, and unique sound-spelling exceptions.

Knowing the Challenges

4. Instructional Challenges

* Linking a Language Skill to a Unit's Content

* Textbook Terrors

- **Curriculum Boxes – Activities for Differentiated Instruction**
  The following collaboration relieves individual teachers of the onerous task of preparing curriculum resources for every unit of study. Teachers work together to create a variety of resources to address the diverse needs of students. The materials provide content accommodations and differentiated activities for students and can be used by teachers year after year. To begin, teachers decide on a content unit and go through the Curriculum Guide to choose areas where students need scaffolds and alternate activities in order to learn objectives and/or literacy skills. Each teacher prepares one/more activities and stores it in a ziplock bag.

- Activities might include
  - DVD(s)
  - appropriate computer CDs and/websites with topic activities
  - tape recorder of a text section (slower, modulated speaking voice)
  - Readers Theatre script(s)
  - Drama Skit(s)
  - Student-made/acted video(s) collaboration
  - photo clips from other sources with simpler sentence constructions
  - related magazines
  - stories or science books of high-interest, low-vocabulary structure
  - redone content information, simpler sentences, explanations, examples
  - sets of laminated content information on sequence cards
  - sets of a master word list with words cut into syllables
  - content objectives on riddle and answer cards
  - scrambled sequence of main titles and subsections from the text
  - short-data research questions with articles/books/texts
  - sets of pictures and matching summarized paragraphs
  - a list with alphabet letters to spell out key words
  - sets of match cards for definitions to words
  - a content data Bingo ready to copy, and question cards
  - thesaurus activity with key words or words in a paragraph
  - related math or science activity
  - related arts or crafts

Best practices involve students kinaesthetically and collaboratively.

How Do I Teach Language in Content ?

1. Look at the 'required standard Curriculum unit' in a new way. Think; words, grammar, discourse *

   Highlight any word, grammar and discourse items in the unit that you think will/could pose a problem for **your** students.

2. In this book, the term 'Content' refers to the main concepts, ideas and facts that are required learning.

   If you are concerned about not getting the Content covered in the **time** allowed, cross out any extraneous information or activities; pare down the standard unit to essential content, and add language skills activities that your students need.

3. In # 1 above, you identified the challenges for your ELLs and each challenge points to the skill(s) **your** students need. Use the 'Difficulty Lists' on the prior pages if you wish, and write in language skills you can teach through this content.

Vocabulary _____

Grammar _____

Discourse _____

Subject Specific* _____

The Language Conscious Teaching Approach to Curriculum

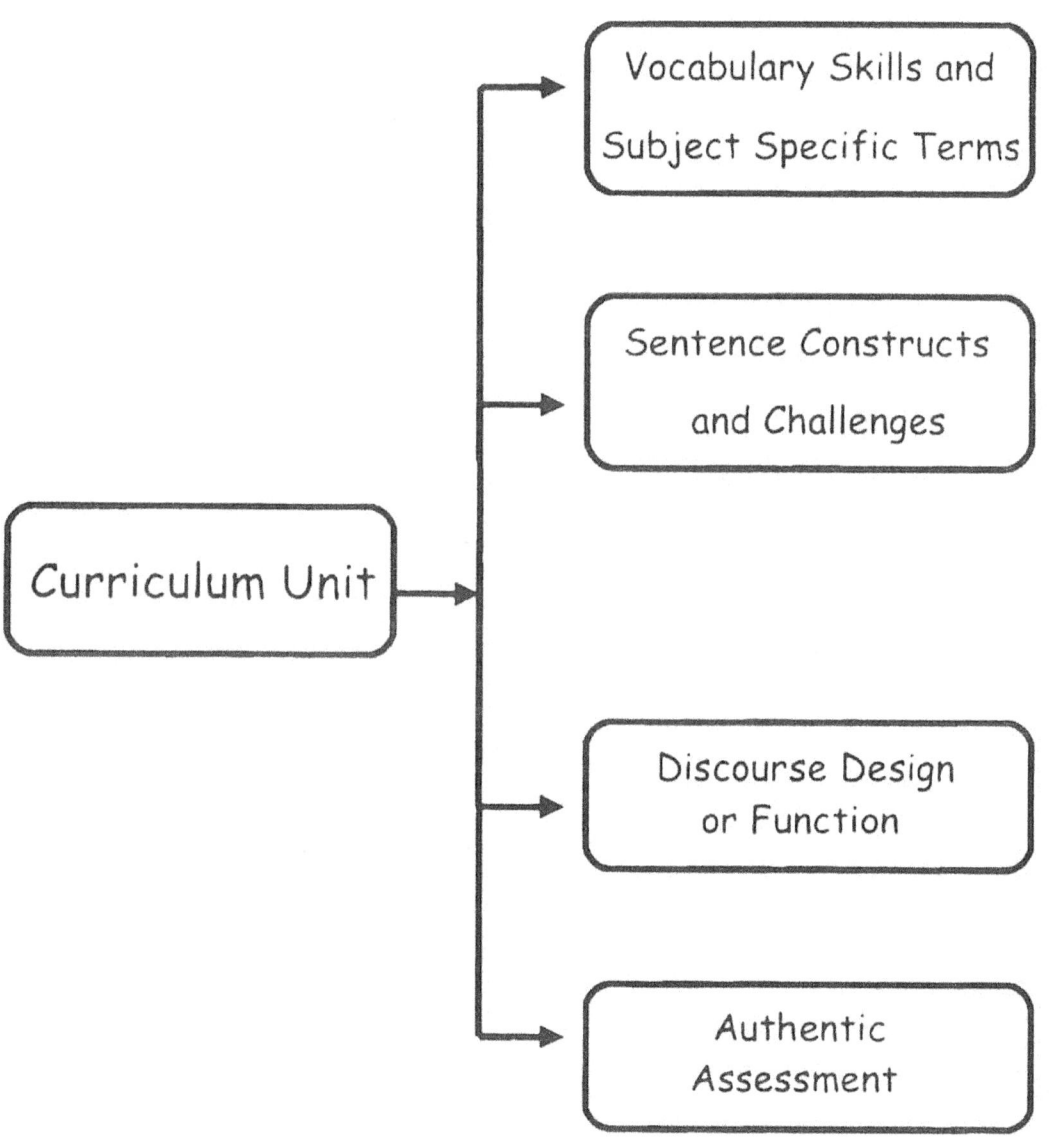

```
        ┌─────────┐              ┌──────────┐
        │ Content │              │ Language │
        └─────────┘              └──────────┘
              ↘      Teaching      ↙

        Information           Words & Grammar
        & Concepts            Discourse Skills
                   Processing

        Topic                 Concept & Abstract Words

        Objectives            Syllabication, Pronunciation
                              Sentence Stress

        Knowledge             Text Skills

        Comprehension         Grammar, Clauses, Idioms

        Application           Function & Procedures

        Synthesis             Note-taking, Summarizing

        Assessment            Test Skills

        Academic              Linguistic
        Competencies          Competencies
```

93

Identify Cultural Dissonance

Scientific and Mathematical content material is typically globally accepted as factual and so there little chance of a cultural mismatch.

When educators analyse Curriculum for instances of linguistic and academic challenges, add an asterisk or a star whenever there is a question of cultural mismatch.

Also add the asterisk if there are blatant or underlying issues of bias, racism and intolerance, even when that example refers to same culture situations such as financial disparity regarding class, poverty, sexism, youth issues or generational discord.

Many issues whether explicit or implicit, are issues that face every culture and generation, and as a result they can provide opportunities for inclusive education, wherein every student can relate to similar matters.

Text Book Learning
Challenges and Solutions

Key Vocabulary, Comprehension and Cognition
Language Learning Backgrounder

English language learners were asked to turn to the first page in their texts for a unit they had already completed. In this sample, grade 6 students worked from a grade 6 History text, and grade 7 students worked from their grade 7 science text. The students paired up to identify unknown vocabulary on that first page. Consider the effect on content and concept learning if students can not comprehend the required vocabulary. The results of this task are below. These ELLs had been in English Immersion classrooms for 3 years.

Grade 6 – History
Unknown Vocabulary

- era
- exploration
- explorer
- explored
- chronology
- occur
- contributions
- milestones
- examine
- gather
- controversy
- conflict
- competed

Grade 7 – Science
Unknown Vocabulary

- define
- list
- describe
- apply
- identify
- observations
- inference
- procedure
- apparatus
- characteristics

Textbook Terrors

Most textbooks reduce your child's ability to:

- 'read between the lines' as unspoken meanings

- construe meaning from long, clause-embedded sentences

- read a text with correct English intonation and/or stress

- understand cultural or historical references/assumptions

- 'get the big picture' because of so many unknown words

- learn correct pronunciation of new or difficult words

- give a grammatically correct response in speech/writing

- cope well with expectations to learn and to be successful on tests and exams.

Students trying to learn from texts can be discouraged and frustrated

Textbook Skills

Teachers must introduce and reinforce text features as useful tools for students to comprehend and locate data. Subject texts use features to:
- organize and present information
- highlight important ideas
- illustrate essential data
- add pertinent, supportive details

> Introduction, Why and What You Learn
> Headings
> Subheadings
> Table of Contents
> Glossary
> Index
> Chapter Overviews
> Chapter Summaries
> Bolded or Italicized Words
> Boxed Text
> Personal Stories or Profiles of People
> Captions and Labels
> Photos and Illustrations
> Cartoons
> Maps
> Charts, Tables and Graphs, Timelines
> Themes
> Websites Reference
> Footnotes
> Bibliography

Student Pair Scavenger Hunt

Text Feature	Page Number
Text Introduction	
Headings	
Subheadings	
Table of Contents	
Glossary	
Index	
Chapter Overviews	
Chapter Summaries	
Bolded or Italicized Words	
Boxed Information	
Personal Stories or Profiles of People	
Captions and Labels	
Photos and Illustrations	
Cartoons	
Maps	
Charts, Tables, Graphs, Timelines	
Website Reference	
Footnotes (page bottom or end of text)	
Bibliography	

Dictionaries May Cause Problems.

Looking Up a Word
Dictionary entries with their unique short forms, pronunciation keys and multiple meanings are often confusing for language learners. It is often more helpful to paraphrase a word and put it in context.

Concept Vocabulary
If a student does not understand the translated meaning of a new concept, then a dictionary activity won't help.

What to Do
Alternatively, a teacher could have language learners obtain an 'explanation' from a same-language speaker as a homework assignment, and discuss it afterwards.

Most urban boards employ translators or other staff who could develop a series of taped translations that explain key curriculum concepts. Lastly, students could be videotaped as a concept or new topic is explained.

Hearing Text Style Genre Subject Discourse for Language Learners

ELLs must hear the cadence of English, the rising and falling of intonation in discourse from an informational text, the stress and pauses in speech that signal emphasis or separate key points in a list, the pronunciation of key words and names.

Student speech activities will be less effective if ELLs are not provided with examples of subject-specific discourse. The ideas that follow offer teachers strategies for providing speech input.

- ✓ DVD movies of topic (context and speech)
- ✓ Video or TV segments (subject-specific)
- ✓ Teacher readings of introduction/sections
- ✓ Audio tapes (slower pace) (10-15 minutes)
- ✓ A guest speaker and/or interview
- ✓ On-going teacher summations of ideas
- ✓ Reading aloud a piece of in-class work before and/or at the end of an assignment
- ✓ Teacher spoken Yes/No, True/False Quiz
- ✓ Teacher reads daily a section of a related story or novel

Language Learning with a Text

For the most part, texts are not geared toward English Language Learners, but to the grade level standards for English Language Arts, or Science, or History, etc. Some elementary basal readers now employ scaffolds in the presentation of their material: highlighting reading notes and questions, spacing of text, including appealing photographs, and clear graphs and diagrams.

Generally speaking, however, the style and presentation of text information requires modification for differentiated instruction. Use these ideas to make text content easier to comprehend.

1. **Write a précis** or summary of each section. Use simple sentence structures, instead of lengthy, complex discourse. Keep these from year to year. They have multiple uses.
   - ✓ Student pair reading first and finally read as a whole-class
   - ✓ Creating a cloze exercise deleting key words
   - ✓ Using the cloze as a test tool
   - ✓ Sequencing assignment if sentences are placed randomly

2. **Review text-skills** at the beginning of each chapter. If text-skills are taught initially then a unit could start with these as standard procedures.
   a) Skim the chapter and predict the topic
   b) Use graphics and section headings as main details
   c) Discuss ideas and compose a brief oral summary
   d) Model pronunciation and translate concept words
   c) Read the first and the last paragraph of a section
   d) Highlight key concept words in sections

Language Learning with a Text

3. **Restate** the prior lesson/concepts to ensure that students link the prior knowledge to the **new concepts**.
    - Rephrase key words to explain an unknown term
    - Make board notes of content objectives
    - Don't make language learners read from a text that is beyond their linguistic competence
    - Use 'expert' groups (Cooperative Learning)
    - Use appropriate 'Curriculum Speak' activities that expand student capacity for discourse
    - Recap important ideas from the lesson

4. **Assignments** from a text
    - Identify and clarify task verbs in any assignment
    - Model and start assignments in class, in pairs/threes so further homework becomes clearer and doable
    - Process steps or stages of lengthy assignments such as research reports, essay-writing or presentations
    - Practice the test styles for the unit through guided lessons – also useful for review

Presentation Styles
Provide Students with Unit Goals & a Summary
Provide Models of Excellence for a Completed Task

Using A Framework to Teach Content

1. Before Reading:

- √ Reduce the number of content objectives to be learned and focus on key objectives
- √ simplify objectives for newcomers, ie; name the nine planets, illustrate an experiment, etc.
- √ Elicit prior knowledge
- √ Invite discussion on the topic
- √ Tell an overview of the selection; oral language differs significantly from written text
- √ Introduce advance organizers; headings, maps, diagrams, information grid, etc.
- √ Go over questions to guide students to important content
- √ Preview text headings, sub-headings, pictures and maps

2. During Reading:

- √ Use directed, guided reading strategies to break down lengthy texts into manageable chunks
- √ Text reading by a teacher not only assists student comprehension of new content and vocabulary, but models proper pronunciation and intonation
- √ Students do the reading together in class; assigning text reading for homework may result in hours of translation
- √ Allow more time for ESL students to read silently
- √ Guide note taking by jotting down key content on the board, which students copy and/or translate
- √ Re-write or adapt sections to exclude lengthy, convoluted text.
- √ Incorporate Scaffolding activities
- √ Provide an audio-tape of reading selection

3. After Reading:

- √ Students use a high-light marker on key ideas, words
- √ Students work together to rewrite notes into full sentences
- √ Students keep a log/journal about what they've learned or didn't understand
- √ Make a cloze exercise from the text deleting every seventh word, or key terms
- √ Show a related video or film
- √ Have language learners work with native-English speaking peers to answer questions or to complete seat work
- √ Have students compose questions about the text content; while sharing these, the teacher selects appropriate ones to write on the board for notes
- √ Use maps, time lines, diagrams, charts or a cause and effect chart as key visuals to simplify large amounts of material.
- √ Have students dramatize sections of a text
- √ Show students an exemplary assignment as a guide, i.e., project, essay, poster, etc.
- √ Go over your marking criteria with students to guide assignment content
- √ DON'T assign text chapters for homework if it means hours are spent on translations
- √ Offer an alternative to written tasks, i.e., poster, outline, time-line, cause and effect chart
- √ Conference with students informally to monitor their general comprehension and understanding of new vocabulary

Teaching Text and Study Skills
Language Skills in Content Learning

Two important language skills that ELLs must learn in writing are also very easy to integrate with everyday content instruction. The two skills are
- Note-taking, writing short telegraphic bits of language, and
- Summarizing, condensing text down to important points

ELLs need to be taught how to write in these styles, and a lesson to guide students through the concepts should be taught or reviewed using the following pages.

Summary of _____

Name _____

Note-taking

Name _____   Topic _____

How to Check on Student Comprehension?

According to research, Dialogue Journals are one of the most effective strategies to improve language learning. These journals are also known as interactive writing.

Curriculum feedback forms offer the same opportunity for students to share their understandings and questions on a given topic. Feedback forms, such as the one that follows, allow teachers to catch comprehension problems right away, and since these forms are not marked, they form a low-risk activity.

If teachers choose to use Dialogue Journals as well, students should use one workbook for this activity only, and it will serve as a record of progress and interventions. Teacher should not make any corrections to the student's writing, but can plan instead a lesson for remediation at another time or during a student-teacher conference.

The student dialogue journal provides one of the rare opportunities for language learners to communicate with a model English speaker. A teacher responds to the ideas as the student writes them, but the teacher can also redirect a student's thoughts and model spelling, sentences, and punctuation.

Identifying Student Needs

> When you can describe a student error, you can prescribe an intervention.

- ✓ Examine a student writing sample(s) and identify errors.

- ✓ Look at an in-class and/or homework assignment. Identify errors.

- ✓ Start to use a student response form to identify problems.

- ✓ Peruse an ELL's yearly student file for pertinent data.

- ✓ Use an anecdotal Observation Record of a specific ELL's use of oral language during a class task

- ✓ Conduct an informal teacher-student conference. Look over his/her work. Have the ELL tell you about the topic, read a sentence from the content sample, ask what is difficult.

> The preceding types of data collection to elucidate student proficiencies are described variously as 'Error Analysis', 'Needs Assessment', 'Targeted Instruction' or 'Assessment Record-keeping'. Using follow-up interventions, remediation and/or whole-class review(s) are forms of 'Differentiated Instruction'.

Student_____ Date _____

What I learned

_____
_____
_____
_____
_____
_____

What I don't understand

_____
_____
_____
_____
_____
_____
_____
_____

Feedback Form

In Our Classrooms

Curriculum Modifications for Language Learners
Grades 4-12
Check √ Did you:

1. Provide a list of key vocabulary.
2. Use key vocabulary activities.
3. Rephrase key terms and ideas.
4. Simplify sentence structures.
5. Use pre-reading activities.
6. Simplify vocabulary in lectures and/or text.
7. Make board notes with the class.
8. Encourage the first language for translations, explanations and bilingual dictionaries.
9. Provide multimedia support and key visuals
10. Monitor student comprehension.
11. Teach text skills, note-taking, defining, giving supported opinions.
12. Provide remediation for missed skills.
13. Allow language learners extra time.
14. Assist with a summary of the content.
15. Incorporate "talk on task" activities, pg. 22
16. Conference with students and give individual feedback.
17. Vary groupings for modeling of language.
18. Display exemplary models of assignments.
19. Refer to relevant cultural information.
20. Attend to equity issues (power status, race, creed, sex).

In Our Classrooms

Scaffolding Content
Creating "Talk on Task" Activities

Language Learners must "practice" using language; They must "interact" with various people who can "model" the words and sentences.

Choose one or more activities from each box to provide students with opportunities to develop, rehearse and enlarge "content" language.

1. Stimulate Talk
- brainstorming
- rough draft notes
- relate prior knowledge
- compose questions
- convey point of view
- think - pair - share activity
- homework question

2. Collaborative Practice
- create dialogues, interviews
- music/create a rap
- surveys
- pro and con partner work
- experiments
- show and tell
- group discussion

3. Refining & Extending
- focused discussion
- refine ideas in writing
- choral reading
- categorizing ideas

4. Discourse & Literacy
- informal debate
- projects
- skits, drama
- announcements
- interview adults
- written report

5. Formal Speech
- public speaking
- oral presentations
- panel debates
- recitations
- school/other class presentations
- Parent Night Presentation
- letters to newspapers
- video production

Rules
- Establish importance of "talk".
- Set time limits on the activity.
- Highlight "best practices".
- Address any problems involved.
- Have a "noise" signal.

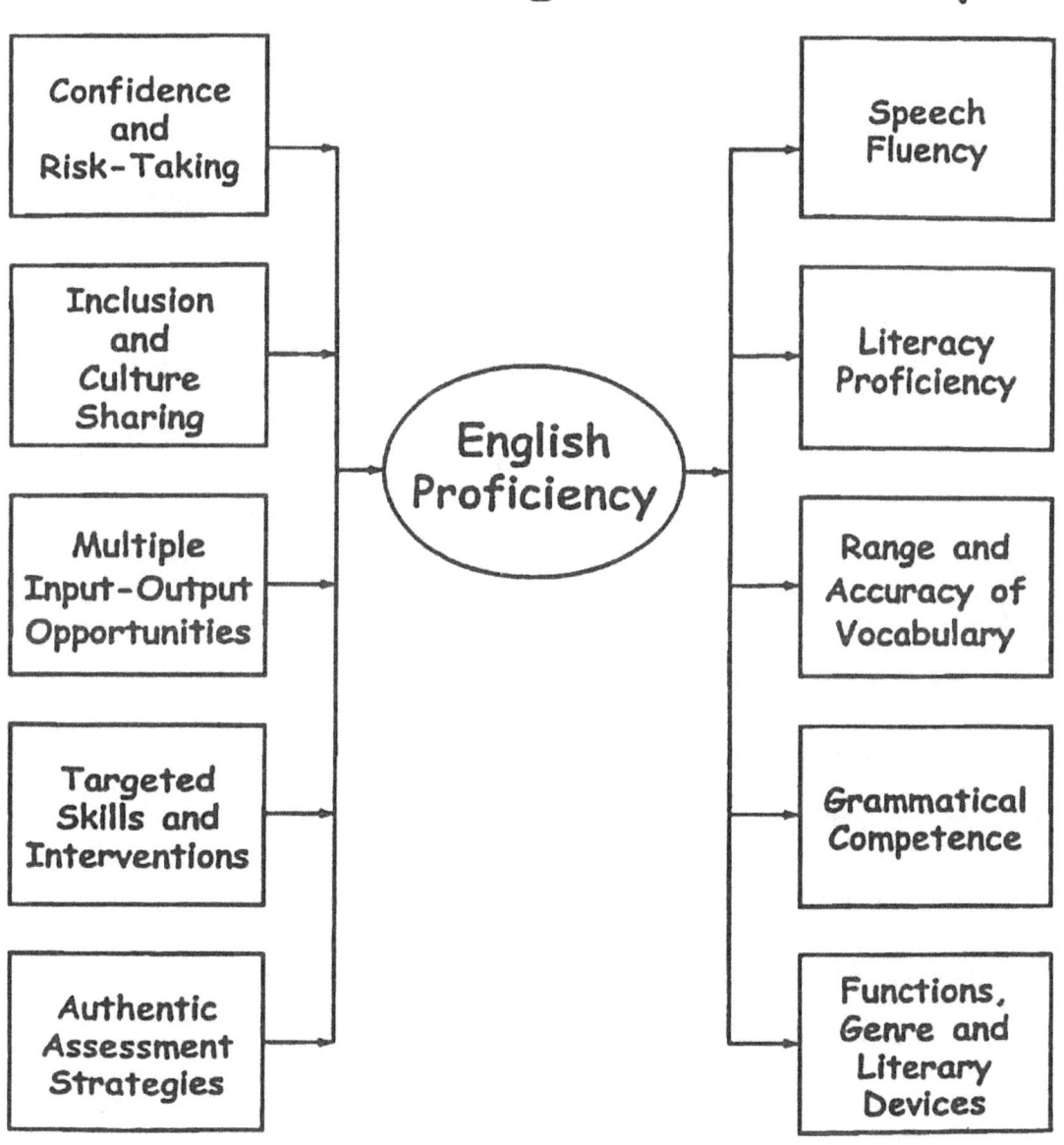

Knowing the Challenges

5. Instructional Activities and Games

The following speaking activities may be used across grades and subjects. They support the learning of graded curriculum, content vocabulary, word-attack skills, correct use of language functions, sentence formations, use of clauses, as well as proficiency with stress and intonation in lengthy discourse in speech and writing.

Games and Activities for Furthering English Skills through Content/Context Learning

1. Initial Vocabulary Level

2. Building Competency at the Sentence Level

3. Discourse Support

4. Learning Subject-Specific Terminology

The Threshold Level Explained

Threshold Level refers to a numerical base of known vocabulary, the minimal requirement of words that an ELL must understand in order to even begin to comprehend English lessons. When relating how ELL vocabulary size is directly related to English usage, Manny Vazquez, former Head of English Language Services for West London Secondary Schools reported,

"Researchers working in this field agree that the 2,000 word level represents the most suitable limit for high frequency words, the classic list of these being Michael West's General Service List. . . .
The first 1,000 words cover about 77% of the running words in texts."

However, Vazquez continues to note other research that found very different minimums of vocabulary requirements for The Threshold Level, quoting a 3,000 and a 5,000 word level, especially for text work.

In addition to a Threshold Level of high frequency words, Vazquez includes another very interesting fact about a specialized vocabulary list for any ELLs intending to do academic work; another 2,000 words that don't even include subject-specific technical vocabulary.

Beyond Key Words or ..... Was the dodo a sitting duck?
Vazquez, Manny, Hounslow Language Service, London, England.

Games for Content Learning

Vocabulary

- Mystery Word
- Happy - Sad
- Chairs
- Password
- Categories
- Pictionary
-
-
-

Mystery Word Vocabulary Game

Every student thinks of a word from a list of Key Vocabulary.

They write the word on a piece of paper.

When called upon students take a turn giving clues about his/her word, so that other students can guess it.

Alternatively, teachers could have the words written already and students have to pick a word, read it, and make up riddles.

Alternatively, teachers may want to allow the student that guesses the word to be the next player.

Happy - Sad
Vocabulary Game

This is a version of Hangman, but a face is used with the last feature being a smile or a sad mouth. Students play in threes.

One student goes first and writes short lines that correspond to the number of letters in the word.

— — — — — —

The goal of the game is to guess the word before you are sad.

Each of the other players takes turns guessing a letter.
When a guess is right the leader prints the letter on the correct dash.

If the letter is not in the word, then the leader starts a head sequence. For every incorrect guess the leader adds the next facial feature to the drawing.

Talk about the method of drawing so the sequence is clear.

i.e., head. eye, eye, eyebrow, eyebrow, nose, ear, ear, hair, mouth

The students have 9 chances to complete the word before the end.

Establish a rule that after a student guesses a correct letter, he/she can take a guess at the word. If it is wrong, nothing happens, and the next student gets a turn.

Chairs
Vocabulary Game

This game is played with multi-syllabic words.

The goal is for students to have one person seated on a chair for each syllable in a word.

The group lines up their chairs, sits, and says the word at a normal speed the first time. Next the word is spoken a little more slowly and for each stressed syllable, that person has to stand up.

Students should repeat this action several times, as the word is spoken. It does get a little silly.

Students choose a word from a box. That student reads the word, figures out how many syllables are in the word and then asks for 2 or 4 or 5, etc. other students to complete his/her chairs.

Keep going until all students are accounted for. Allow students 10 minutes to prepare their chairs. Then the whole class gets to watch while other groups present.

Password
Vocabulary Game

The goal of this game is for students to guess a chosen word.

The teacher writes content words on cards, and a student takes one card from a pile.

That student must not tell or show the others. A teacher might want the student to whisper the word to him/her just to make sure the students can read the word.

The student turns to the audience and says a related word that will help the students guess the word.

Usually whoever guesses the word gets the next turn.

i.e., **rock** – hard – outside – throw – stone

    photosynthesis – process – plant – leaves – oxygen

Categories
Vocabulary Game

This game requires a more extensive list of words. Therefore a teacher might use a text page or a worksheet with written text, or a novel, or story that students have completed.

First establish the Categories, for example, Parts of Speech; nouns, adjectives, verbs, adverbs, and prepositional phrases.

The categories might also be people, places, or events.

One student comes to the front and chooses a word, or points to a word in the text so that only the teacher can see it.

Then the student says to the audience, "Categories."

The audience guesses the category, and then take turns to find and state a word in that category from the text, until the right word is spoken.

Pictionary Vocabulary Game

The goal of this game is for a team member to guess the mystery word or topic from a sketch. There is a 3-minute time limit.

The teacher should have a deck of content words or ideas from which students pick. Students may use an easel or the board.

At a given signal the student quickly sketches a picture that will help his/her team members guess the correct word. If they accomplish this, the team gets a point; if not, no point.

Spinners

Students love to create spinners and use them with other students. The spinners must be copied onto sturdy card stock so they will actually spin – you don't want it bending out of shape after 2 spins.

Students will fill in the sections with compliments, adjectives, future forecasts, Valentine's sayings, etc.

You can make a spinner with alphabet letter to spell our words or to say a word that starts with a letter.
You can write curriculum questions or to define terms.

Students will outline the spinner sections using colors and markers after the written work is completed.

If possible, laminate the spinners after or have students cover theirs with clear, tacky paper from the Dollar Store.

Students ought to show their final work to the rest of the class.

Required Vocabulary
through   on top   beside   on   around   between

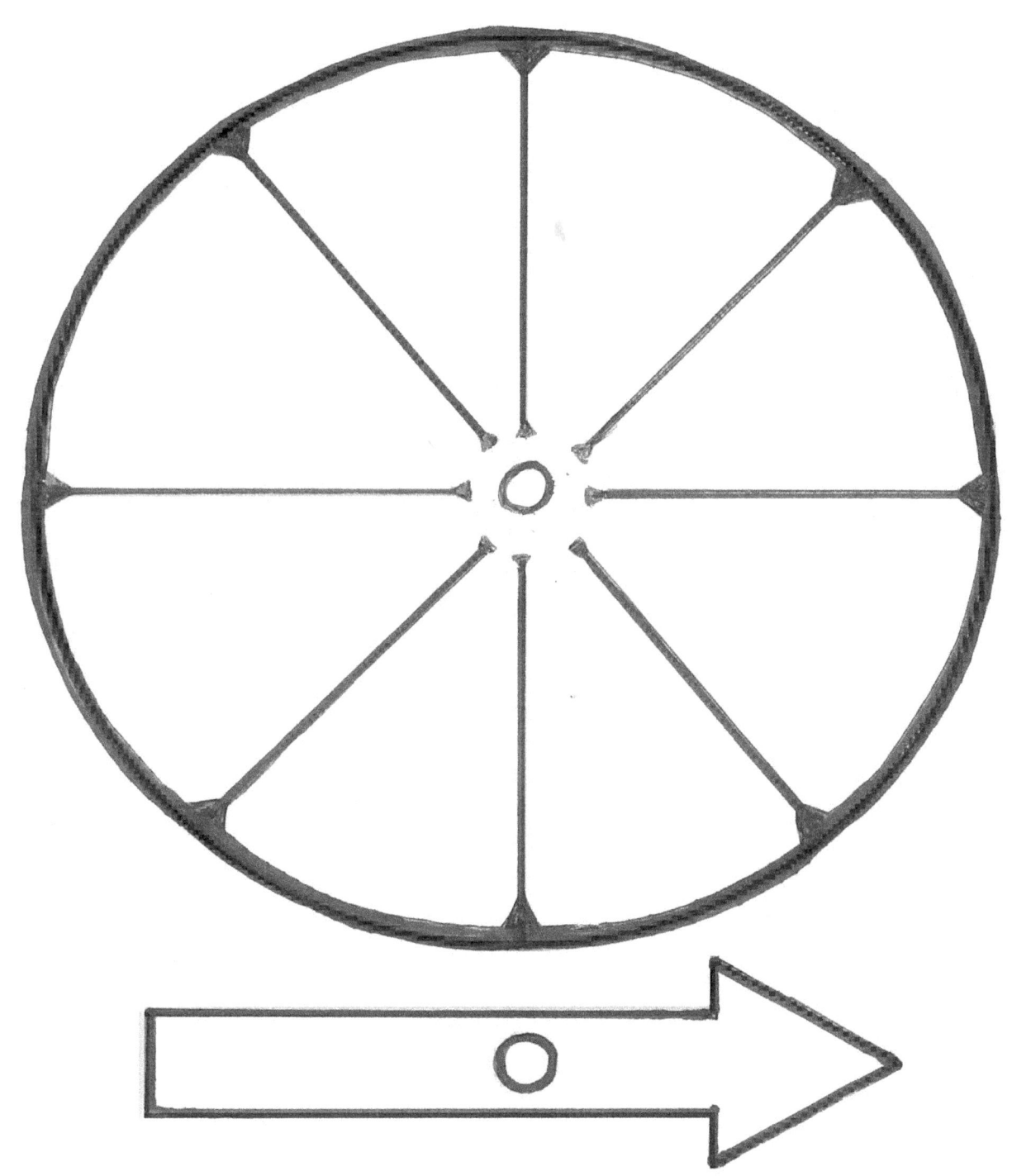

Suffix

Read these verbs and their nouns. Say a sentence for the nouns.

describe	descrip<u>tion</u>
identify	identification
multiply	multiplication
add	addition
subtract	subtraction
invent	invention
pollute	pollution
imagine	imagination
celebrate	celebration
destroy	destruction
inform	information
decorate	decoration
introduce	introduction
graduate	graduation

Word Relatives

Example: science   scientist   scientific

Create a list of word relatives from the unit.

_____
_____
_____
_____
_____
_____
_____
_____
_____
_____
_____

Prepare to talk about the variations in class.

Matching Games
Vocabulary Review and Speaking

Here is an easy way to create many different card sets for language Matching Games. Assign students to work on the sheets of blank pair cards for a given topic. After that teachers may select card pairs that are neat and drawn clearly for copying.

Topic Suggestions

Mathematical Signs or measurement terms to words
 % # $ X ½ < > - etc.

Verbs - match a present tense to the past tense word
 go - went

Contractions - match contractions to their full words
 won't - will not

Health Terms - match a health problem/illness to a body picture
 sore throat - neck, concussion - head

Adjectives - match a new adjective to a hand-drawn picture
 soft - pillow, sweet - juice

Holidays - match an event or celebration name to a symbol
 Mother's Day - mom/flowers/card

Countries - match the country with the nationality
 Sweden - Swedish, England - British

Compound Words - match the first word to its second part
 sun - set, car - pool, rail - way

Prepositions – match prepositional words to their illustration

Parts of Speech – match these to a word example
    Noun – tree, Proper Noun – Maple, Abstract Noun – pain

Characters – match a name to a description or role
    Laurier – First French-Canadian Governor
    Wibur – the pig that Charlotte tries to seve

Locations – match a place to an activity/verbs
    Hospital – operating, examining, Bank – save, deposit

Prefixes – match the prefix to the correct word
    un – comfortable, im – patient, co – operation

Student Names – match student's first names with his/her last
    Alan – Chan, Jenny – Gonzales, Mr. – Smith

Small Pairs Cards

Riddle/Question & Answer/Complete the Sentence Subject Card

Brainstorming

> Brainstorming is a technique to develop ideas quickly. It's often used as a problem-solving activity within a small group but also as a method for students to come up with ideas for a task.

* In a brainstorming session, students write/speak related thoughts spontaneously. This must be a free thinking activity to allow for creativity, new ideas and to generate connections.

* There is to be no criticism or sarcasm. In the end, students will decide on or evaluate which of the ideas they want to use.

* Only single words are used, or if necessary a phrase/notation.

* The activity has a short timeline – perhaps 5 minutes or so.

*Afterwards, students can color-code or categorize the thoughts so they have a framework to express information.

Brainstorming is often called Webbing and visa versa.

The following pages illustrate the technique.

Topics for Brainstorming:

⬆

pencil or pen - elicits uses, colors, made from wood
books - teach/learn, titles, types
school - teacher, principal, library, recess, grades, etc.

Food
lunch/fruit/vegetables/meat/ice cream flavors, etc.

Animals
pets/those living in the forest/zoo/jungle/swamp/ocean

Special Days
Words for Valentines/Halloween/birthdays/holidays, etc.

Things Made of
wood/plastic/rubber/steel/clay

Thanks Found in
stores/hospital/school/restaurant/home, etc.

**These topics require more thought:
pollution/the future/history/emotions/the brain etc.**

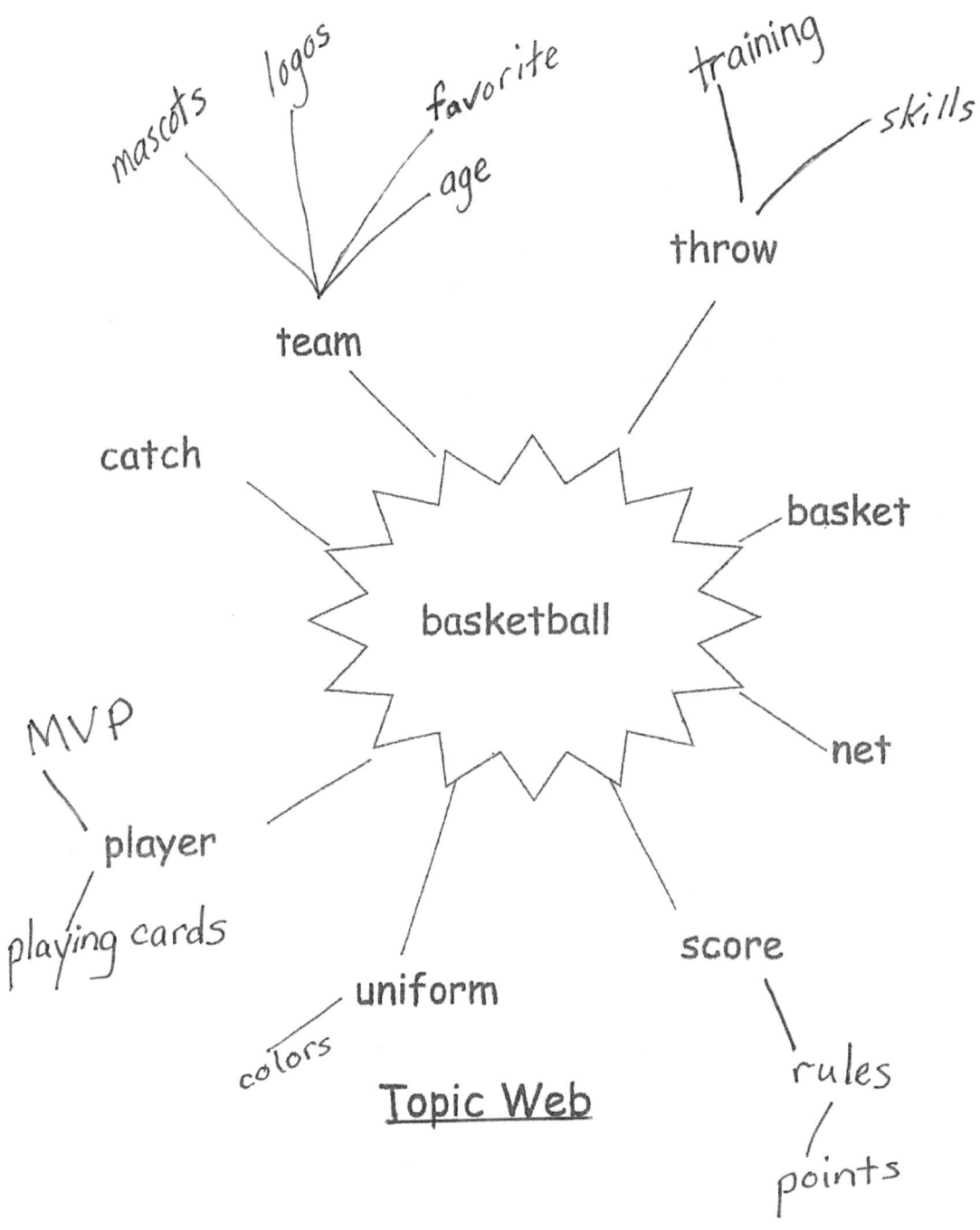

Topic Web

Topic Web

Adding Details in a Paragraph

You have practiced this idea with your teacher;
now, write 3 details about one of your brainstorm topics.

Topic _____

Detail #1

_____
_____
_____

Detail #2

_____
_____
_____

Detail #3

_____
_____
_____

Assignment: Write one paragraph using this work.

A Cloze Assignment
Using Key words and Content Information

What is Cloze?

Cloze refers to content-based text, or teacher-made information, that has significant words deleted or omitted. This type of cloze activity is more useful than one with every 5th or 7th word taken out. Deleted words could be subject specific vocabulary which would review both vocabulary and context information for ELLs. Cloze, used with ELLs, is an indicator of student comprehension.

MadLibs, commercial kids' activity books, often delete English Parts of Speech like nouns, verbs, tense, adjectives, etc. Cloze can be developed for even basic level readers. An easier cloze activity would be to provide the beginning letter for each missing word or show a picture of the missing word

Students fill in the blanks to complete the information.

Spelling

1. Write the words you know from the spelling list.

2. Pick out five more words to learn.

3. Read each word to the teacher or another student.

4. Translate each new word into your language. Use a dictionary from home.

5. Divide each word into syllables. Use a red pen.

6. Look up the meaning of each new word in an English dictionary. Copy the meaning beside the word.

7. Write each word in a sentence.

8. Study the words at home.

Timeline; Sequencing Events Activity

Facts

? Who	? Did What	? Why

Writing a News Report - The 5 W's and How

Title

Who

What

Where

When

Why

How

Jeopardy Sentence Game

In this activity, student groups prepare a list of questions about the content. The teacher will have to give a lesson beforehand to model the types of questions from the list below. The teacher will choose which 10 questions are best for each category.

The categories are chosen by the teacher and reflect content and genre style of information.

Categories usually are listed as dates, people, cloze, riddles, places, finish this statement, definitions, objects, etc.

A panel of 3 students is chosen, plus a person to tally the points.

The teacher (or a good reader) is the 'Moderator'. The categories are listed on the board, and the Moderator has the questions for each category. Each panel member gets a turn to choose a category, and answer the question. If the answer is correct, that student gets 10 points. If the answer is wrong, another panel member may try to answer and get the 10 points.

The game is over when all the questions are done, or when class time runs out.

Jeopardy Board

100	100	100	100	100
200	200	200	200	200
300	300	300	300	300
400	400	400	400	400
500	500	500	500	500

Step up!
Sentence Game

This goal of this game is for all students to be able to answer content questions prepared by their teacher. The questions should be short and factual.

In this game, students form teams of 10, and the person at the front of the team's line must answer the teacher's question. The teacher decides how many teams to have. There must be at least one student to keep score.

If the first student in the team can answer the question, they step forward. Stepping forward makes it easier to see which student responded first.

If the student, who stepped forward first, answers correctly, then that team gets 5 points. If the answer is wrong, each of the other teams gets 5 points. After each question, the first person in each team goes to the back of the line, and a new team member gets a turn.

Puzzles
Sentence Game

The teacher enlarges a page from a text, or a worksheet of information from the curriculum topic. A content picture with related text is a good option too. An example might be the water cycle or types of environmental pollution, etc.

The goal of this game is for small groups of students to piece together the sentences so the text is correct.

Student helpers can assist teachers in the preparation of this activity. The text should be enlarged a lot so that all group members can read it, and the sentences pieces are easier to handle.

The text sentences are cut where each sentence ends. These are not sentence strips, but sentence chunks.

This activity can be saved and used from year to year if the sentence pieces are glued onto Bristol board and laminated.

Each group receives an envelop of the text sentences and works cooperatively to complete the puzzle.

Who's My Date/Friend Sentence Game

Four students play this game, which is similar to the Mystery Guest. This time one student asks questions about three hidden people. The questioner should not see the other individuals.

This time the hidden people are intended to be a date (if they are older students) or a friend (if they are younger students).

The teacher prepares the names of the 3 persons, and they wear these on their chests, clearly visible to all.

The one questioned must ask only 6 questions, two for each hidden date.

After that, the questioner must choose number 1, 2 or 3 as a date or friend.

The three dates/friends are personalities from a book or unit.

True or False Sentence Game

Similar to Step Up, this game involves three teams of students each forming a line. The goal is to get the most correct answers.

There are 3 large cards, each with 'True' on one side and 'False' on the other.

The teacher prepares a set of content facts in statement form. When a statement is made, the first person from each team turns around and holds up an answer for everybody to see.

Whichever person answers correctly, their team gets a pre-determined number of points.

Sequencing Subject-Specific Content

The following Sequence activity idea works just as well in Science, History, or English, as it does for story and novel work. Once a mixed sequence is written in any subject, it can be re-used every year.

Students form groups of three.
Triad groups ensure inclusion, yet offer opportunities for ELLs to listen to repeated pronunciation of the topic vocabulary.

The sentence strips actually provide ELLs with practise speaking structured English discourse. There are few other ways for ELLs to actually learn to use this 'academic' English unless they are doing Reader's Theatre or simply reading out loud from the text.

Try to ensure that at least one of the students is a stronger reader. The goal of this activity is to review both the topic information and to use the required language. A strong reader is able to support ELLs with reviewing the ideas so they all can use the content language to complete the task.

Important information from a unit of study is written 'out of sequence' on the sentence strips on the following page. The students are told they must speak about the work while they decide on the correct sequence. Then they glue the strips in sequence.

During this activity, a teacher should have enough time to record observations about the speaking abilities of several language learners.

Correct this Sequence

Sequence Strips   Group Names

Short Sentences or Phrases

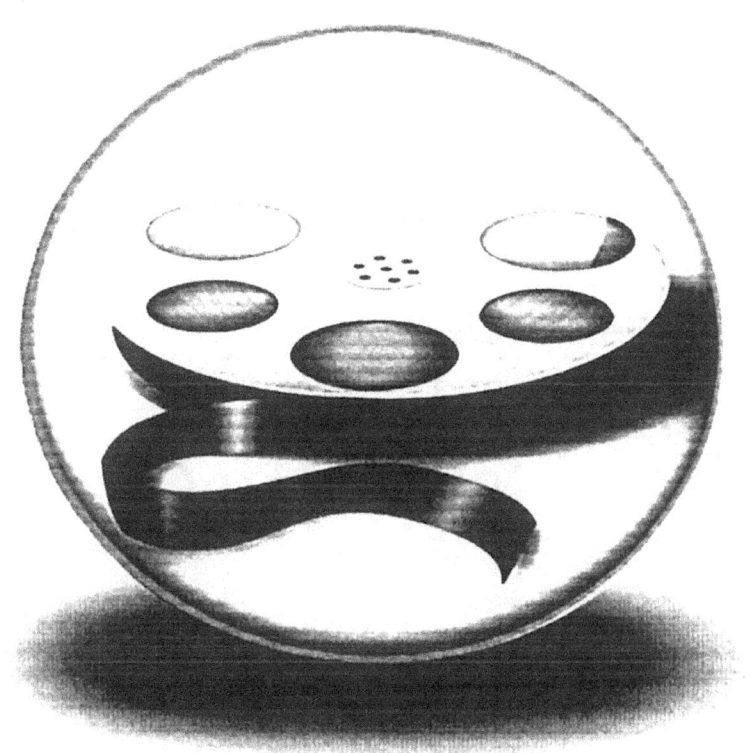

Try Movie Frames
for Students to Sequence, Illustrate and
Highlight a Topic's Main Events

Prepare Power Point Presentations
as a Concise Overview and/or Summary

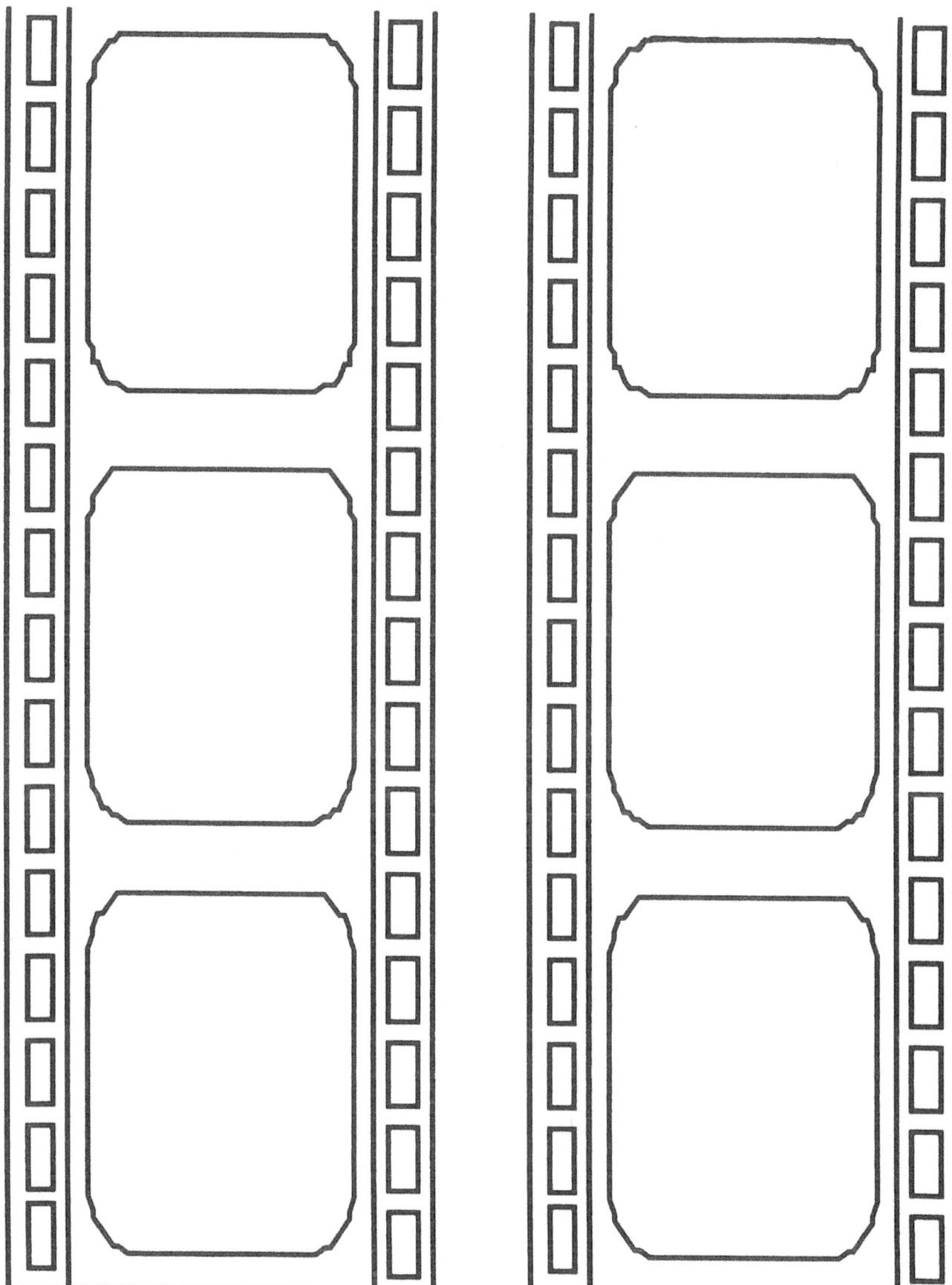

Character Study
Main Character

- Draw the main character.   • Write his/her name.
- In the boxes, write an adjective or personality word about the character on the line.
- Finally, write proof from the story.

Other Characters

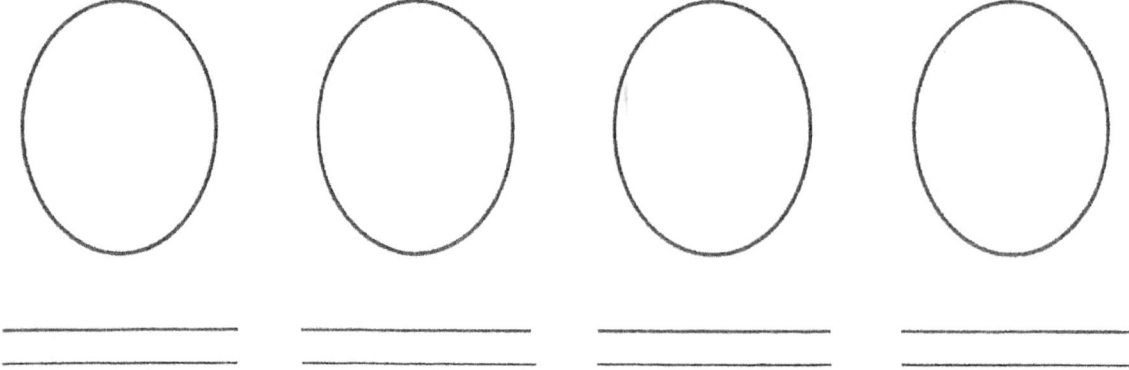

Are you looking for a better word?

1. Go to this website www.thesaurus.com/
   and type in - say

2. Now, go to www.merriam-webster.com/thesaurus
   and type in - say

3. Then, go to www.synonym.com and type in - say

4. Which site do you like better? _____

5. There are so many words with a similar meaning but only a few are right for your work.

   Pick the word that you think fits your word the best.

For example
ran - jogged   raced   dashed   sprinted

saw - looked   noticed   observed   examined

6. Look up a word and write synonyms below it.

   My word = _____

   Synonyms _____   _____   _____

Sentence Stress

WatchKnowLearn.org

Okay, this is not a game - but I just had to add it in case you weren't aware of it. WatchKnowLearn is a super-directory of over 50,000 free educational video links that are organized by subject matter.

You'll have to sign up on their website even though the service is free for teachers, parents and students everywhere.

Everything on the site can be translated into Spanish or Chinese by clicking the language button at the top right.

Rather than spend a lot of time clicking on the various subject areas, I went to the Search bar and typed in Compound Words first and then later I searched for Persuasive Techniques. Both times I was pleased with the range and quality of offerings. A great many had animation with text and voice or song overlay - all of which is attractive and fun for younger students. Why turn yourself upside down to get attention - just try a pertinent video.

English Speech
Sentence Stress in English

English speakers stress nouns, verbs, adverbs, adjectives and question words in sentences, but usually do not put any stress on pronouns, prepositions, conjunctions or helping verbs (modals).

Intonation refers to vocal pitch. In English, we use intonation to convey emotions, highlight important information and much more. "You did that?" "It's a beautiful day, isn't it?" ". . at nine o'clock."

Intonation changes in phrases and clauses within a sentence. Even pauses add meaning or assist with clarity of a message. We use rising and falling intonation patterns to create the rhythms of English. Some Asian languages use pitch to create a different meaning. In Mandarin, 'na' spoken with a rising pitch means to take, but spoken with a falling pitch, 'na' means to pay taxes.

Don't attempt to teach such linguistic features to Elementary students. In order to increase your ELLs' proficiency with spoken English, become a model of informal language in discussions, conversations, questioning, rhymes and jokes. Model more formal and academic speech through reading, drama or multi-media.

Another very useful and direct approach to helping ELLs with intonation in lengthy sentences or using content discourse is to write out several important sentences relevant to the content, and have students look while you read the section with emphatic intonation. Read again but have students repeat the intonation of each section after you. Next, guide students in dividing the speech segments with a slash at pauses, and marking the rising and falling patterns with line strokes. After you read a final time, ask students to try reading the piece with proper intonation.

Focus on One

'Focus on One' is a strategy to bring a child into active participation. This technique works well for a student who is consistently and noticeably quiet and reserved, who is not actively engaged but is attentive. Using Focus on One, a teacher focuses on giving that one particular child special attention for a designated time, say one week, and observing any changes. The attention would include; eye contact, saying his/her name as you walk by, interaction, time, a touch on the shoulder - all the signals that say to the child, "I see you, I like you. You're special to me. We invite you into our space because you're one of us." This is a very non-threatening, non-invasive strategy that never forces reticent children to be in the limelight, but welcomes them on a personal, non-intrusive way. The Focus on One is usually very successful in bringing that child into active engagement with peers and learning situations.

Games for Content Learning

Sentences

- Questions and Answers
- Mystery Guest
- Charades
- Jeopardy
- Step Up
- Puzzles
- Who's My Date?
- True? or False?
-

Question and Answer Match Sentence Game

Prepare an equal number of questions and answers regarding the Curriculum topic.

The goal of this game is for students to find the partner with the matching question and answer.

When partners are matched they line up along the front and side of the room.

Finally, each pair says their questions and matching answer.

Card Sequencing or Matching

Make activities for students to practice learning data or language. Copy the cards on stock card. Write the activity. Laminate the cards. Use the cards to make activities:
- ✓ To sequence historical/novel events, experiments, recipes, . . .
- ✓ To match characters with facts/actions/personality/rationales
- ✓ To match new vocabulary to definitions and text examples
  explore – to go looking or searching – England explored new lands.
- ✓ Proper Nouns – WW1, Allies, France, England, Duke Ferdinand . . .
- ✓ Abbreviations
- ✓ Word Relatives i.e., explore, exploration, explorer
- ✓ Other ideas

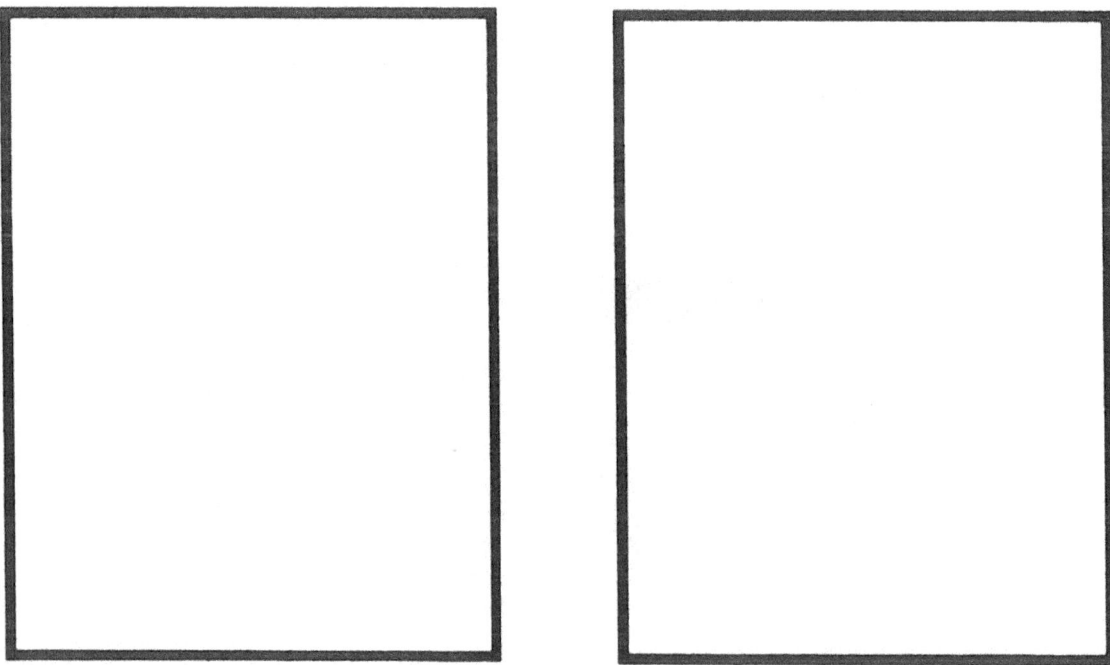

Riddle/Question & Answer/Complete the Sentence Subject Card

Charades
Sentence Game

The teacher prepares a list of actions (verbs) in context from the sequence of the topic being studied.

The goal of this game is for students to guess the action or activity of the player, who uses only mime or gestures to act out the message on the card.

The student who guesses correctly gets the next turn.

If no one can guess the message, then the player chooses another card and tries again. However, teachers may want to change the rules so that every turn is by a new student.

Mystery Guest
Sentence Game

The teacher will prepare names of the major characters in the unit of study or in a story.

The teacher will choose four students; one will be the mystery guest and the other three are the panel that asks questions. They all sit on chairs at the front of the room, but are hidden from each other, or perhaps the panel turns their chairs away from the guest.

The goal of this game is to guess the identity of the mystery guest by asking yes/no questions.

The mystery guest will be hidden to the panel, but the rest of the class should be able to see everything.

The teacher puts the identity card on the chest of the guest.

The game ends either when 20 questions have been asked, or if a panel member guesses the guest's identity.

How to Write Quotes

Direct Quote – Use , " "   Indirect Quote – Use that

=

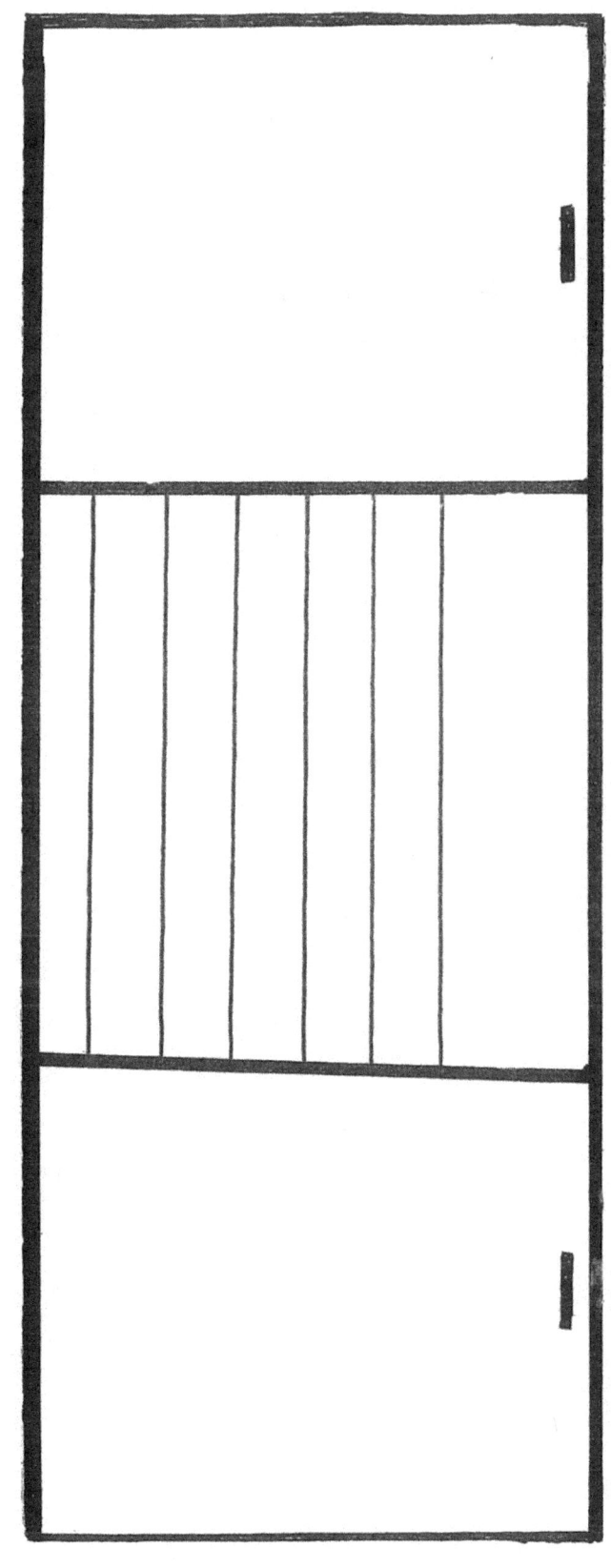

Subject Content Questions and Answers

In space 1, teachers will write a question concerning the study unit. There should be enough questions/variations for class partners.

In space 2, student pairs discuss and then write in an answer.

In space 3, students draw/create an icon that represents the idea.

Inform students that the combined marks for space 2 and 3 reflect the correctness of the answer and the creativity of the artwork.

Plot and Time Lines Form

Use the following sheet

- ✓ to sequence a video or movie
- ✓ to present a timeline in visual format
- ✓ to list main events of content or a story
- ✓ to tell a story
- ✓ for a comic depiction

How to use the following sheet

- use a former student's work to model the activity
- make multiple copies of the form
- decide the type of text (point form inside the frames or written text under each frame)
- point out the overlap to glue the frames together

Action Strip/Storyboard

Use for Time Lines/Plot Development/Sequence

Storyboard – Video Production/Plot

Names_____

Curriculum Speak
Surveys, Polls and Questionnaires

In-class surveys, polls and questionnaires offer English language learners multiple occasions to review vocabulary, and use the discourse and language structures in a given subject. These are low-risk activities since students will not feel singled out. Every one else is speaking too.

Student surveys can be structured:
- ✓ to practice specific vocabulary or language skills
- ✓ to practice using longer discourse
- ✓ to review content facts or details

For example
What do you think . . .?	(Opinions)
Why did Laurier . . .?	(Past tenses)
Have you ever . . .?	(Perfect tenses)
Which words describe . . .	(Vocabulary)
Add another detail/reason/word to my list . . .	
Tell me how. . .	(Explaining specific detail)

Curriculum topics can also be made into surveys
- ✓ by asking about motives, details, characters, results
- ✓ by having students reply to true or false questions
- ✓ by getting students to choose an opinion, a reason, sequence

These content-related speaking assignments provide essential opportunities for students to hear and practice the discourse style (genre) and key vocabulary of that subject. This oral 'work' lays the foundation for success in written tasks and test(s).

Name

Survey Question

Who did you ask?   Answer

In Our Classrooms: by Mary Meyers

Short Answer Survey

Work with a partner.

Question ↓	_____ your name	_____ partner's name

Sequence

> In English, events are usually told in a linear fashion. They are listed in order: first to last, next, then, after that, finally, etc.

Children learn about sequence through songs, nursery rhymes, stories, TV and videos and also from their daily schedules.

The following activities help teachers present the concept of sequence and its corresponding vocabulary as a literacy tool.

First   second   next   now   then   after
after that   afterwards   when that is done   at last

Use the words to tell the sequence.

One Saturday morning ….

Then …

After that ….

At last …..

Next …

Finally ..

Sequence means put things in order, first to last.

so   then   after   next   finally

How to Make Maple Syrup

 First,

 Next

After that,  <u>boil</u>

Then,

when it's done, you can

First   second   next   now   then   after
after that   afterwards   when that's done   finally

Use the words to tell the sequence.

 First, I bought a Tee-shirt. Then when I got home, I saw that it was made of plastic fibers

_____ washed it

 _____ the dirty water with the plastic fibers goes down the drain and into the lake or rivers.

_____ fish and birds eat it and they could die.

Finally, even though the water you drink is cleaned, some fibers are still there, and they go in your body.

Writing Know How

Use the following vocabulary and activities as an oral introduction before written work. Have students listen while you enunciate each word and provide a sentence. Ensure comprehension and translation if needed.

1. Adding Ideas or Sequencing a Topic

also   first   second   third   and then   next

for example   for instance   as well as that

another   furthermore   moreover   as well   too

besides   not only that but   in fact   in addition

finally   lastly

2. Students use a word and volunteer ideas for this topic –

- How To Be A Good Parent

3. Lastly, students volunteer ideas for the following topic and copy the paragraph(s) as you write it on the board.

- How to Stay Healthy

Cohesive Devices - Joining Words

1. Read these words with your teacher:

   then   after that   next   so   also
   because   but   finally   and   at last

2. Read this story and fill in the correct word.
   I went shopping with my mom on Saturday_____
   I needed new shoes. We went to the mall and
   _____ looked for a shoe store. There was a
   small store _____ it didn't have anything I
   liked. _____ we walked around some
   more. _____ , we saw a big store with
   so many great shoes. I tried on six pairs of running shoes. _____ , I tried on some sandals
   for summer. _____ , I picked out the ones I
   really liked. _____ , it was my mom's turn to
   get shoes.

3. With your teacher's help, write another story using the cohesive devices.

4. Now, write your own paragraph on the back using the joining words.

   by_____

Discourse
Language Complexities in Lengthy Spoken or Written English

Explanations enhance our own comprehension: when we explain something to someone, we understand it better ourselves... For instance, students who explained textbook material <u>performed better</u> on tests of that material than those who studied it twice. Prompting students to explain is a powerful learning technique especially in partner/small group settings. Even explanations comprised of even simple sentences and phrases served just as well since re-phrasing, back-tracking and self-correcting behaviors assist in clarifying information.

By Maria Konnikova | April 7, 2012
.scientificamerican.com/literally-psyched/2012/04/07/hunters-of-myths-why-our-brains-love-origins/

Correcting Student Errors
in Pronunciation and Grammar

We don't want to take away from a student's spontaneous answer in class, and we certainly don't want to discourage an ELL from taking risks.

Guidelines

In speech
- If the meaning of a spoken comment is affected by the student's word choice or pronunciation, clarify it or model the correct word in your response to the student's contribution.

In written work
- Correct grammar in response to a student's written work, but do so judiciously. Make sure your corrections are attuned to the student's comprehension level.

- Do not mark all over the student's work and lastly, any feedback is more effective if the teacher meets one-on-one with the student.

- Teach students to write on alternate lines so you have space for corrections.

- Teach students your editing signals. i.e., adding /changing a word above the line, arrows directing a student to another way to say something or your comments, adding corrections in a color, etc.

Curriculum Modules
Activities for Differentiated Instruction

- This idea involves a collaboration between teachers to relieve them of the onerous task of creating a variety of resources all by themselves. The materials compiled in this collaborative endeavour will provide content accommodations as well as many activities for either in-class or homework.

- To begin, teachers of the same grade decide on a content unit and choose areas where students usually need scaffolds to learn concepts, and to use them in specific language and literacy tasks. Then each teacher will prepare an activity to store in the curriculum box. Finally, teachers present the activity so everyone knows exactly what's in the box.

- Your Curriculum Topic box of activities could include:
    - an audio recorded section of text using a slower, modulated voice
    - an audio of text/worksheet concepts using conversational language
    - appropriate computer DVDs and websites with topic activities
    - in-class survey sheet using topic concepts/vocabulary (opinion/facts)
    - Readers Theatre script(s) about the topic concepts
    - Drama Stills - students plan a 'still' for key information (retain photos)
    - a prepared list of video stories/segments that students will prepare
    - photos, maps/diagrams with key vocabulary for writing sentences
    - magazines, visuals, color, high interest or easy library books to read
    - re-write of content information with simpler sentences, explanations
    - sets of content information on cards, laminated for sequencing
    - sets of key words with matching syllable sets - or matching definitions
    - content objectives as a riddle and answer activity for partners
    - cards to match main titles to subsections on the topic
    - short-data research questions with a computer URL of articles/books
    - sets of pictures that match summarized paragraphs
    - sets of syllable parts to spell out key words from a prepared list
    - sets of key vocabulary for cursive writing practice
    - Bingo with content answers in the boxes and questions as calling cards
    - a thesaurus activity with key words in an informational paragraph
    - a related math or science activity to reiterate the words/concepts
    - related arts, crafts or a media activity

Games for Content Learning

Discourse

- Top Story

- Who Said That? (Listening Tape)

- Ring, Ring (Phone Conversation)

- Help Line (Phone Request & Advice)

- Issues

- Skits

- Prioritize, Cooperative Learning

- Expert Teams, Cooperative Learning

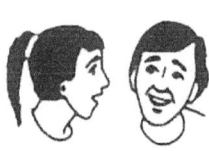

Top Story
Discourse Game

The goal of this game is for small groups of students to create a news headline that is short and snappy for a paragraph of key events in a curriculum unit.

This activity requires students to help each other read and understand an important piece of information. After that, the group must summarize the ideas into a headline, known as a Top Story.

Teachers should use the same paragraph for all groups, and then have students share their versions. This sharing helps students understand summarizing and the technique of telegraphic speech.

When students are really competent with this game, teachers could prepare paragraph cards of different sections of a unit.

Alternatively, teachers could ask students to develop a paragraph from a chapter or section heading.

Who Said That?
Discourse Game

The goal of this game is for small groups of students to decide which character would have spoken the comments heard on a tape.

Teachers need to prepare a list of characters, and the ideas they might have spoken about. Student helpers could assist with taping different voices.

When the student groups are ready, they must listen to each section of the tape and choose the speaker from a prepared list of characters. If the tape comments are spoken quickly and contain many clauses, it should be played twice.

The Daily News

_____
Topic

* Sequence the major events on the reverse side.
  Circle one event your group will report on as News.
  Have the teacher check over your group's decision.

* Write down all the information you need to tell:
   date and time, place, people, event, cause, results,
   interviews, opinions, facts, pictures, map, etc

* Prepare and practice a group presentation or video.
  Have one announcer introduce and conclude it.
  Each person must announce a part of the News.

* Speak clearly and loudly. Use intonation.
  Be professional.

News Team Presentations

Topic _____

1) Overview - Issue   Team Members
News Announcer states the topic
Introduces the experts
Experts offer their opinions
(In my opinion, I believe that . . ., I think . . ., As I see it . . .)

2) In the Spotlight   Team Members
News Announcer restates the topic
Introduces the reporters
Reporters talk about one section/part
(Currently, At this moment, Right now, I can tell you that . . .)

3) Viewpoint   Team Members
News Announcer summarizes the topic
Introduces the experts
Experts offer their advice
(I'd suggest, They should, They ought to, It's important to. . .)

Ring, Ring
Discourse Game

The goal of this game is to identify the two characters who are speaking to each other on the phone.

Student pairs are given a dialogue of two people from the content unit. Students practise the phone call so they develop comfort with phrasing and intonation. Each pair knows who their speakers are.

After a set time, the student pairs take turns presenting their dialogues on a set of cell phones. The other students must guess who the speakers are.

Help Line
Discourse Game

The goal of this game is to identify which character is calling the Help Line for assistance or advice. This is supposed to be a tongue-in-cheek parody of the main ideas from a unit or story/novel.

The teacher needs to prepare a series of speaker cards in which a main character pretends to call and request advice.

The speaker cards are shuffled and one is given to each student group. One of the students reads the speaking text, and the rest of the group tries to identify the speaker. One student in each group must practice the text for the class presentation of Help Line. He/she should try to memorize the speaking part and add emotion to the part.

When the groups are ready, each group speaker presents the call, and the class guesses who the caller is.

The teacher cards should refer to something that happens or something that poses a problem in the content unit.

For example, Red Riding Hood calls to ask directions, and explains why she needs them.

Curriculum Speak
Different Points of View, The Problem

These forms require students to consider different perspectives that people bring to a problem. Initially, students may need to be encouraged to expand on, or to explain, their own reasoning. With repeated use of this activity, however, students will concentrate on reasoning and creative thinking. Use this activity for student problems, Environmental Issues, History, Novel Study, even Math problems. If possible, ensure one of the partners or several group members are able to provide English support for ELLs.

When students use the Different Points of View form, it is important to establish whose points of view should be expressed. For example, will it be two other students, two characters from a story, two countries perspectives, etc.

Issues Interview
Fluency in Spoken Discourse

Reading fluency comes more readily when students have a personal experience with the topic. In this activity, students talk about information they received during an interview.

Consider the ideas in the curriculum unit, and have students help list issues about the topic. Each student then chooses one of these issues as the base question for his/her interview. Students could interview a relative or church member or another adult. However, it is best to ask students whom they want to interview.

1. Students record the issue they want to ask about.
2. Tell the students they must 'jot down' notes to help them remember details.
3. Students need to practice retelling the answer. In terms of language skills, this activity will help students learn to use indirect speech. For example, He said that . . .
4. Suggest that students include the emotions and feelings that the person had about the issue.
5. Inform students that when feelings and emotions are included, listeners relate to the information.

_____

Topic

Each students gets a copy of this sheet. Review the idea
of pro and con. Get every student to talk. Everybody should help
each other with ideas. Students take notes in point form only.

Pro	Con

Different Points of View

A.

_____ thinks   _____ thinks

B.   What I Think   **?**

_____
_____
_____
_____
_____
_____
_____
_____
_____
_____
_____

The Problem

_____
_____
_____
_____

Solution #1

_____
_____
_____

Solution #2

_____
_____
_____

Solution #3

_____
_____
_____

Solution #4

_____
_____
_____
_____

- Which solution seems the best to you? Be prepared to say why you chose the solution you did.
- Put a red star ★ beside the solution you favour.

Reproduced from *Teaching to Diversity: Teaching and Learning in the Multi-Ethnic Classroom* by Mary Meyers.

Create a Rap, Song or Poem

* Group Names _____

* Day 1

    Prepare a point form summary of the major ideas and events on the back of this paper and hand it in.

* Day 2

    Try composing a rap, a song or a poem. Decide.

* Day 3

    Hand in a clear draft of your composition.

* Day 4

    Prepare and practice a presentation, 3 minutes
    You may use movement and include 'rhythm' background (snap/instrumental) etc.

* Your date to present is _____.

Curriculum Speak - Drama

The purpose for using drama as a strategy for content learning does, in fact, create the perfect model for ELLs to acquire language, content and discourse skills in speech. Dramatic activities support and encourage students to use and extend their existing oral language while involved in creative, social, context-driven situations. Drama also creates what Vygotsky refers to as 'the zone of proximal development'. With so much language going on in dramatic activities, ELLs have multiple occasions to acquire language that is slightly above their current proficiencies.

English Language Functions

Just as important though is the style of English speaking that is modelled and used during this peer-related activity. The language used alternates between informal and formal speaking. There is a great deal of 'student talk' that performs particular functions in English; functions such as the language of planning, cooperating, sequencing, getting a word in, decision-making, and building social relationships and leadership skills.

Assessment

Dramatic tasks do not simply provide a bit of amusement in a text-driven course. They offer wonderful opportunities for assessment of individual student strengths and talents that show as an end result of shared creative expression, original thinking, and social and group skills demonstrated through cooperative behaviours.

Student Skits as Content

Provide titles from a content unit or allow students the choice of creating an idea of their own, as long as the group checks it with the teacher.

* Students work in groups (5 or less) to develop a skit.

* During the first lesson, students decide on their title and then brainstorm ideas to form an outline.

* Each student must be at least one character.

* Inform students that they may use props and costumes but not backdrops.

* The skit should be 5 - 10 minutes.

* Practise in class to accommodate student schedules.

* Decide on a due date and write it on the board.

Scenario Cards

Use these cards to write scenarios of the most important events. Students must sequence the cards and check it with their group. Each of the 6 groups will prepare one scenario for presentation.

Prioritize
Think-Pair-Share, Cooperative Learning

Use this activity for review of main sequences and content issues.
Prepare 4 to 6 main ideas from a content unit.
Students will work to prioritize these ideas from most important or valuable, at the top of the pyramid, to less important.
They will work on the form on the following page.

First, students will have an opportunity to read, think and prepare ideas by themselves. This is in preparation for verbal work.

Secondly, students will pair up to read, share, discuss and edit the ideas. Tell students that discussion is imperative because they must reach a consensus, which will be written on the following form. Both names are included on the worksheet.

Finally, as a whole class, students share their ideas and make a decision for the final prioritized list.

New vocabulary includes:
- Priority
- Prioritize
- Consensus
- Reach a consensus
    and
- Content vocabulary

Priorities

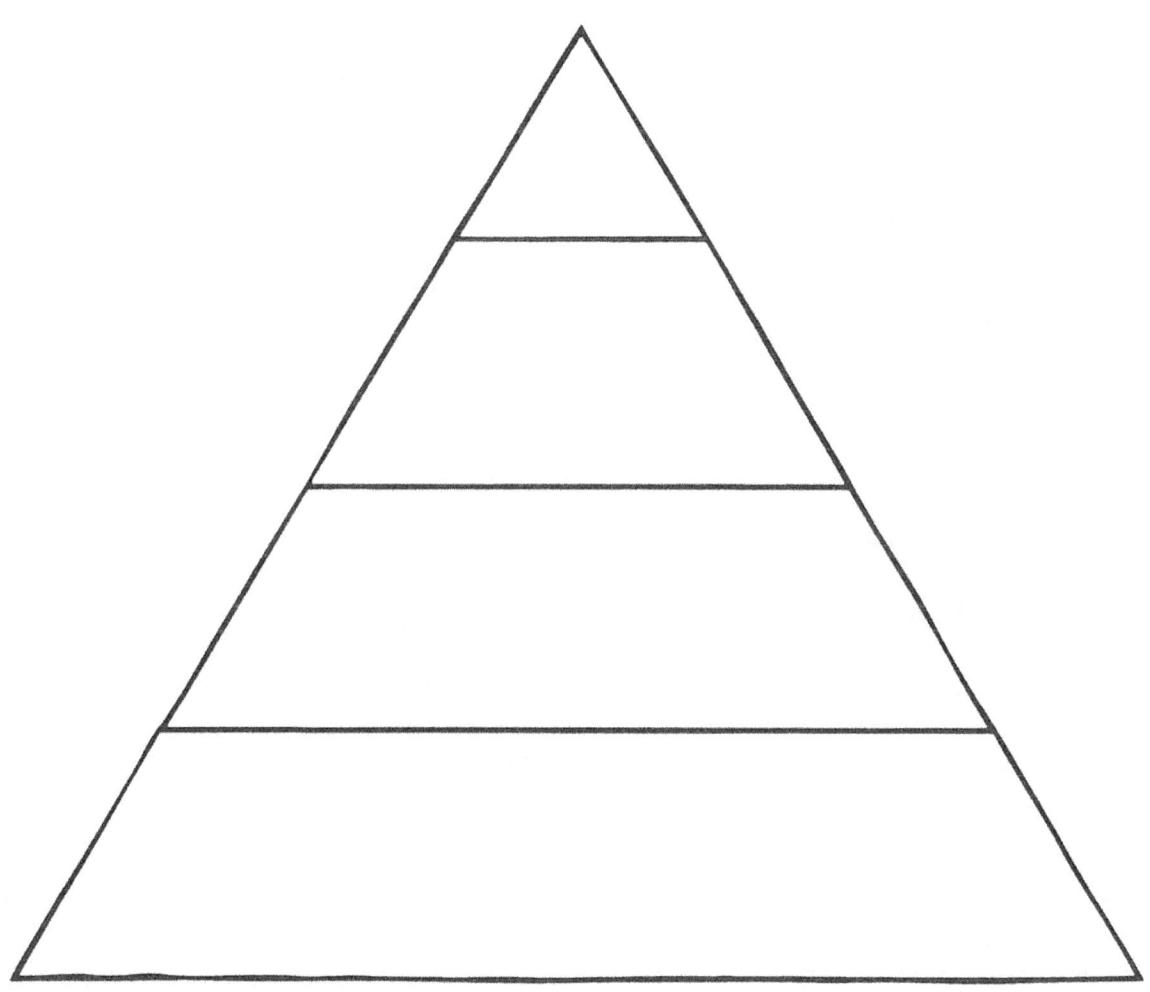

Cooperative Learning, Expert Teams Discourse

The goal of this activity is for groups of students to be engaged in and supported while learning one aspect of a topic. When all the groups reform back into their original teams, each student becomes an expert in their area of discussion. The end result cannot be achieved without every student's expert input. This activity requires discourse at various levels of difficulty.

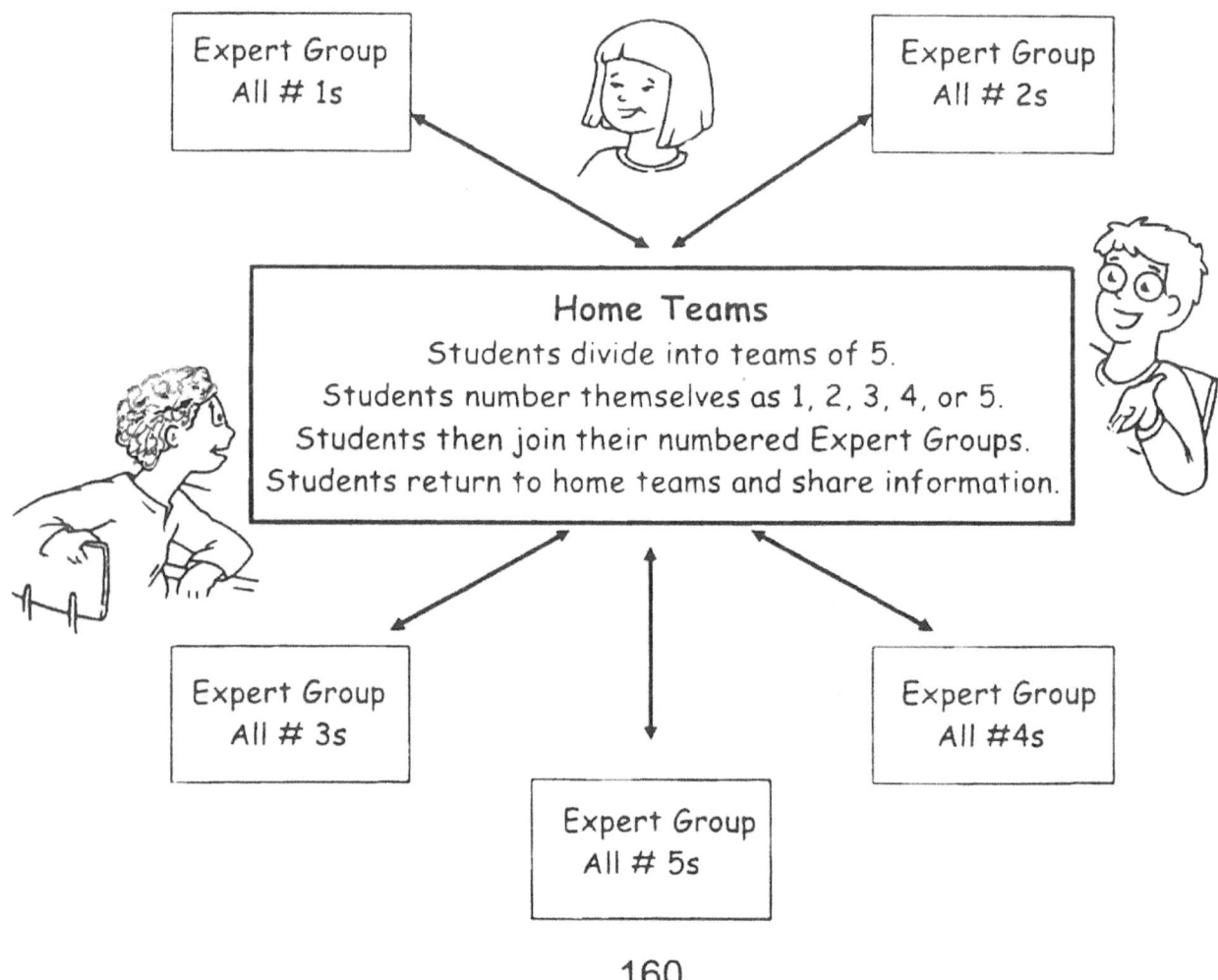

Identify Behaviours in Talk Activities

Students will learn to identify, name, portray and discuss a variety of behaviours in oral communication.

How to play
1. As a whole class, students are introduced to the vocabulary for the behaviours. After that students are encouraged to provide examples of both oral and body language for each behaviour. THIS IS A BOISTEROUS, FUN-FILLED ACTIVITY.

2. Groups of students are given different topics to discuss. 3 students are called aside from each group and given a behaviour card to exemplify during their group's discussion.

3. The behaviour cards can include
    * Interrupting - Excuse me/Yeah, but/ uses hands
    * Bossy
    * Social Misfit - can't get a word in, too close proximity
    * Summarizer - always summing up the main ideas
    * Complimentary -encouraging, saying nice things, no ideas
    * Pretender - uses a variety of pauses, phrases and body language to sound clever and thoughtful
    * Clarifier - always asking or repeating what a speaker said
    * Bored - facial expressions, gestures and noises
    * Task-master - tries to keep everybody on task
    * Argumentative - opposes everybody's ideas

4. Groups are encouraged to show the rest of the class and students may take turns.

5. Discuss.

Cooperative Learning

Research shows that Cooperative Learning improves:

- student achievement
- race relations
- social interactions and...
- language acquisition

Cooperative learning involves many wonderful strategies beyond interaction in partner and group tasks. The best strategies provide for "talk on task" and literacy activities that include students at varied skill levels.

This is just one.

What other cooperative learning strategies do you know ?

Think-Pair-Share

This easy strategy provides time for students to process, practise and revise their thoughts in English.

Think-pair-share works across subjects.

1. Pose a question and ask students to think about the answer by themselves first. You could also ask students to write their answers down, which encourages students to revise their initial thoughts.

2. Next, ask students to pair up with one partner and tell each other their answers. This oral step will help students to decide on corrections.

3. As a whole class, share the answers and reiterate correct ideas. Write a summary together or individually. Whole group sharing and revision supports and extends concepts and language and is very non-threatening for ESL students.

Speech Presentation Practice

Speeches in front of a whole-class can be terrifying for some students, and many ELLs have particular anxieties about their perceived inadequacies in language, task assessment and cultural expectations.

Students will be more relaxed about the task of preparing a speech and the presentation skills involved if the task is practised (initially at least) in the guise of small group activities.

Prepare a student rubric for a mini-data research, limiting the topic, organizing ideas, adding details, creating visuals and learning time management with due dates.

Prepare another set of activities that help students understand, identify and practise the following presentations skills in their small groups and finally discuss and exemplify the points in class.

1) Pronunciation
2) Word stress and volume
3) Intonation and voice modulation
4) Eye contact
5) Facial expressions and nervous behaviours
6) Body language and posture
7) Pacing or speed
8) Clarity of voice
9) Clarity of information
10) Use of props or visuals to convey meaning

Speech Presentation

Topic _____

Student _____ Mark _____

Delivery   Remarks

1. Pronunciation
2. Clear Speech
3. Appropriate Language
4. Audience Contact
5. Evidence of Practice

Content   Remarks

1. Introduction
2. Details
3. Conclusion
4. Clarity
5. Organization

Reader's Theatre Discourse

The goal of ELLs creating a Reader's Theatre presentation is to develop speaking skills using text from content.

1. Tell students that they will develop speaking parts about the content so that it becomes a Reader's Theatre that can be performed as if it were a radio program.
2. Help students list main characters.
3. Introduce the idea of a narrator.
4. Divide students into groups to read different sections or to develop a script from different perspectives.
5. Each group must have a narrator and parts for everyone. Students may also create sounds to accompany the story.
6. Groups will then need class time to rehearse parts.
7. Discuss with students the importance of intonation, since Reader's Theatre uses voices only, no acting.
8. After several practices, students can perform the story for the class or put it on a tape recorder like a radio program.

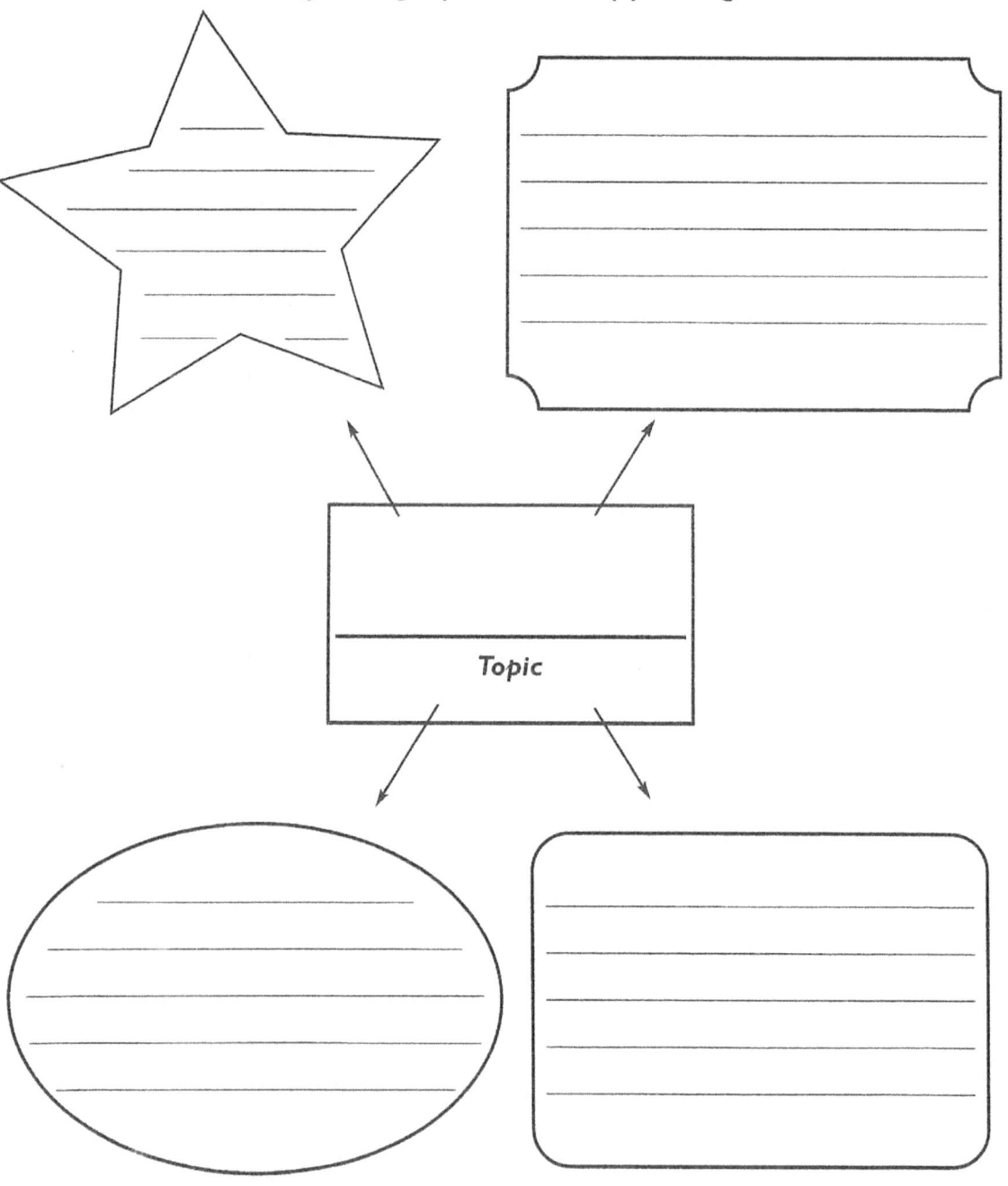

Details   Details   Details

Use for Problem Solving, Expanding Topic Ideas, Environmental Issues, History

Cohesive Devices
Joining Words
Connecting Words

The titles may be different, but the concept is the same; longer sentences are formed using conjunctions (and/or/but) and clauses (whenever, while, so that).

Specific joining words are used for particular 'functions' of English. For example, listing reasons or details in a piece of writing would use the following connectors; also, in addition, because, so, etc. Specific English Functions and related vocabulary are dealt with further on in this resource.

In a piece of writing, be it a paragraph or an essay or a report, students must become aware of a variety of English sentence structures such as simple sentences, compound sentences and dependent and independent clauses – though younger children do not need to remember the terms or identify them. Older students will understand the concepts and 'how to' at grade level.

The best way to introduce the concepts involved with longer discourse is to model them through reading to students and playing with language: something older students enjoy as well. (Title: Fortunately Unfortunately as well as story books that have a pattern or sequence structure)

Teacher Reference
Linking and Joining Words

Linking and joining words help a reader to understand the connections you are making in your thinking and writing. Linking words are usually placed at the beginning of the sentences. Below are some examples of words that show when you are changing from one point to another.

(Teachers, I'd suggest you have students practice on at least one activity for each set.)

To Add Information
again	additionally	along with	besides	in the same way
likewise	moreover	as well as	not only ... but also another	
also	furthermore	further	equally important	
in addition	what is more	for example		

To Conclude or Summarise
in short	consequently	accordingly	finally	in conclusion
due to	to sum up	in summary	for this/that reason	
as a result	therefore			

To Emphasise a Point
in particular	truly	for this reason	indeed	particularly
again	mainly	to emphasize	in fact	with this in mind
especially	to repeat	specifically		

To Clarify
to put it in another way   in view of   in other words   to clarify
to put it more simply

To Give a Reason
in view of   due to   given that   since   as a result of   on account of

To Show Similarities
both   similarly   in the same way   just like as   likewise
also   equally   in the same manner

To Contrast or Show a Difference
however   while   otherwise   in the meantime
even though   alternatively   although   if   but
nevertheless   another possibility   in spite of   despite
while   on the other hand   still   conversely
apart from   rather much as   as opposed to

When Making a New Point
next   as for   it follows that   with regard to
with reference to   turning to   given that

To Show Time
before   at   prior to   by the time   meanwhile   after   finally
while   whenever   immediately   about   until   during
as soon as   at which point   soon   since then   as long as
in the meantime   later   next   afterward   subsequently

To Show Sequence
First/firstly   second/secondly   third   finally in conclusion
to begin   once that's done   tomorrow

Source:
Education Drop-in Centre 2013
http://www.somers.k12.ny.us/sis/main/writing/transitional_words.html

Curriculum Speak – Discourse Skills

This game reviews Cohesive Devices and builds a student's facility with discourse skills. Cohesive Devices are sometimes called signal words or transition markers. Small groups of students improve their listening and speaking skills in this low-risk activity.

Copy the master set onto different colours of stock card paper, then cut and "baggie" the sets.

Review or teach the vocabulary beforehand. Have students translate unknown words. Teach correct pronunciation by marking word stress, and intonation practice.

Play one or two games to demonstrate how to play the game.
The game is played in small groups of 4-6.
Students shuffle the story cards, and then turn them face down.

Students choose a member to start. This person begins to tell a story. The start must be one or two complete sentences.

The next student must turn over the top card and then add to the story using the word(s). At this point, student creativity and humour can be stressed and enjoyed. The student shows the card to the others and then keeps it afterwards.

Students must continue telling the story using the next card that is turned over in the pile. However, if a student turns over the word "Finally", that student has to make up a quick ending for the story. That is the end of the game, unless there is time or interest to continue the game. Expect lots of laughter.

Tell a Story Cards

| And then |

| After that, |

| However, |

But then

Although

So

Instead

After a while

Eventually,

Yes, but

In fact,

Nevertheless,

Most importantly

At the same time

Even though

Content Bingo

Intent
This game forces students to speak with other students using the language of the genre and content knowledge.

Preparation
Make up questions about the content of a unit of study. Write them in each box of a BINGO form. Copy enough sheets for each student.

Procedure
Introduce the game and distribute the Bingo sheets. Tell students that they must walk around the class and ask different people the questions in the boxes. Whenever someone answers the student writes that person's name in that box.

When a student gets answers in a line, across or down, or answers in the 4 corners, that student calls out "Bingo".
Give the student a simple prize.

Rules:
No interrupting, no shouting or no pushing.
Students may only ask one person for one answer.
Students can answer their own questions only once.

Content Bingo

What is Communicative Competence?	How many ELLs are in your classroom?	What's the optimal age for learning a language?	What is Cultural Dissonance?
Give an example of oral sound blending.	What is Cloze?	Why is syllable stress so important?	What does ELL mean?
What is Discourse?	What is the difference between an immigrant & a refugee?	What is 'output'?	Explain a language function.
What is Comprehensible Input?	What is tolerance for ambiguity?	What are the two expressive skills?	Explain 'missed skills'.

Bingo Play Sheet   My Name is_____

Cut and paste the vocabulary items randomly on this blank form

Sites for Curriculum Instruction and Messages

Translations for Students or Parents

translate.google.com

http://translate.reference.com

www.microsofttranslator.com

Making a Text Section Easier to Understand

http://rewordify.com

Student Editing Program

grammarly.com - Grades 4/5 up, Free download. Very popular

Whiteboard

Copy/scan any pages and visuals that you want to use and then put them all into a single file. Move any page to the Whiteboard system when you want to use it for large group instruction. Phone your school board Tech person to arrange a visit to help you set it all up. Maybe he/she'll have other support ideas and even bring out some copies of board purchased materials as well.

Language Buddies

Language Buddies builds on the basic premise that student pair interactions provide positive experiences for both individuals. Most schools are familiar with pairing an older student with a younger child as a reading buddy. Although pleasurable, being read to is a receptive skill only, that of listening. Without question-answer interactions and re-readings of the same story, ELLs miss opportunities to develop vocabulary and extend comprehension.

> A buddy leads a group through an activity.
> Talking is essential to the task.

With Language Buddies, an older student works with three or four students on any variety of activities, from using magnifying glasses to book making, from answering text questions together to a spelling activity, to playing a Bingo game of opposites. Using Language Buddy groupings, a teacher may direct an activity to address a specific need that students have for vocabulary, skills development or curriculum support. Language Buddies is also an excellent strategy to provide 'differentiated instruction'. The non-threatening guidance from an older language buddy may be used to support all students, from special needs to enrichment.

With buddy support, students will find their work tasks seem easier, and as the students gain confidence, they will participate more in their own learning.

An key element in the dynamics of the Language Buddies program occurs when both the older buddy and the individual students see and hear the progress made as a result of their interactions. This dynamic promotes an authentic sense of achievement and enthusiasm.

> An activity becomes prescriptive
> when a teacher uses it to address student needs
> for language or literacy skills.

The Language Buddies Effect

* offers English models and translation support

* provides non-threatening and low-risk circumstances

* may be used to target student needs

* links oral language and literacy skills while learning

* gives multiple opportunities for content or text learning

* promotes a sense of achievement and enthusiam

What Happens With Language Buddies?

A buddy leads a group through an activity. Talking is essential to the task.

ESL students improve their fluency using "talk" activities.

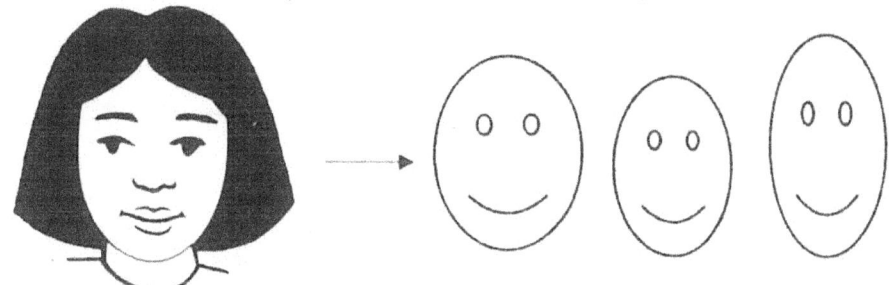

The more vocabulary students learn, the more language they have to comprehend new ideas and skills.

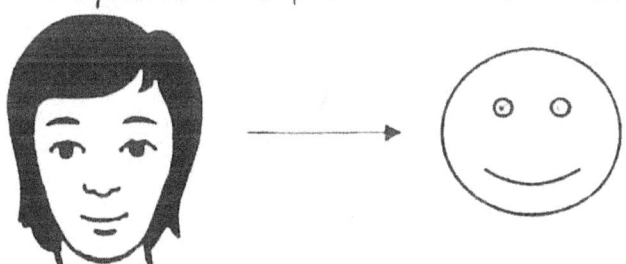

Special needs and remedial students are supported by the verbal guidance and leadership of a language buddy. Work becomes easier, success becomes the norm and students grow in confidence.

You may want to group your class by language, remediation or skills needs. It is up to you to arrange for as many, or as few, buddies as you feel are right for you.

Language Buddies

Q. How does Language Buddies support students in Curriculum?

A. Teachers can set up the activities so that the older student guides a small group of students through a task that involves content knowledge and/or literacy learning.

Q. How can I simplify the process of instructing every student leader about what to do?

A. Prepare cards with content activities, and keep them from year to year. To review content, have the buddy lead ELLs through a homework activity or use a prior class task. In this way, ELLs are supported in a review of the content and of the language in that context. A leader could read parts of the text, practice pronunciation, or use one of the content games in this guide.

It is a good idea to have a selection of activities at different grade levels, even word games to practice word-building, plus science objects, board games, word bingos, etc.

Sample Tubs	Matching Activities to Needs Primary Class
Group 1 3 times a week ALPHABET SKILLS	- Play matching pairs, small to capitals - Sequence alphabet manipulatives - Use computers to show font styles - Alphabet BINGO
Group 2 Four times a week SCHOOL VOCABULARY No English	- Play the 'What's Missing?' game - Make a school picture-word booklet - Play the game with new objects - Play school object BINGO - Let a student call the words
Group 3 3 times a week Color Words Literacy	Make picture-word booklets - Spell colors with cut letters - Play 'What's missing with words - Re-read booklets
Group 4 3 times a week Fine motor skills Concrete to abstract	- Free choice with variety of puzzles - Beading with shoelaces - cutting shapes for headband - roll plasticene to cover letters - tracing activities
Group 5 3 times a week Enrichment/Review	- Play picture verb bingo (present tense) - Start to use past tense - A student gets to be verb caller - Choose one of these students to do bingo with ESL students another time

Sample Tubs	Matching Activities to Needs Junior Class
Group 1 Twice a week Syllable Skills	- Divide spelling words into syllables - Clap out a list of multi-syllabic words - List 2-3-4-5-6-7 syllable words - Rules for double letters, single vowels - Make a set of cards cut into syllables
Group 2 Four times a week Past Tense Verbs Basic English	- Play verb BINGO past tense - Play the second verb BINGO set - Let students call cards and sentences - Cut out magazine pictures for verb words in the past tense, and make a class book.
Group 3 Twice a week Abstract Nouns	- Continue a list of abstract nouns - Find examples in magazines - Make picture-word booklets - Read each other's booklets
Group 4 Twice a week Review letter wtg. 'I would appreciate. . '	- share 'Free Stuff For Kid' books - Show sample letter format - Write letters for mailing - Show form for addressing envelopes - Write a 'request' to the principal - Make up sentences for requesting something. i.e., Could you please, etc?
Group 5 Twice a week Spelling Support	- Make up riddles for the week's words - Say a sentence for the words - Divide the words into syllables - Play "Hangman" - Pre-test and correct errors

Language Buddies
Grade 7-12

Cooperative Learning Replaces Language Buddies

Middle and high school curriculum demands and timetables do not suit Language Buddies.

Cooperative Learning activities support
- Students born here who speak another language
- Students who require remediation or support
- Students close to or at grade level
- Students who need extra motivation
- Racial harmony
- Skills learning

Learning Task	Skill Taught	Pair/Group Work
Text Info.	- recall - sequencing events	. movie frames . timelines
Novel Study	- understanding cause and effect - essay wtg	. graphic organizer . paired wtg
Essay writing etc.	- stating pro and con etc.	. graphic . expert gps . paired wtg

Knowing the Challenges

6. Assessment; What and How

> "The key to success isn't the assessment you use. The key is the actual service you're providing. You have to take a closer look at your program and say," Are these programs really addressing the language learners' needs? Are they really developing English proficiency?" I think those programmatic questions have to be answered before you have any meaningful discussion about the assessments."
>
> Gary Hargett, Northwest Education Newsletter, North West Regional Educational Laboratory, Portland, USA, Spring 2006
> www.nwrel.org

Authentic Assessment

Considerations for ELLs

> Assessment should be descriptive
> (what a student can do) and
> prescriptive (what a student needs to learn).

Teachers assess students to decide

- Components to teach and where to begin
  This crucial knowledge of a student's language proficiency levels including literacy will inform your instructional techniques and indicate the necessary adjustments.

- The amount and type of support a student requires
  ELLs will require a modified program that includes attention to linguistic development and methods that improve content learning. If a student has missed prior schooling, or even grades, more appropriate supports should be added that complement classroom adjustments (ESL classes, bi-lingual tutors, a Language Buddy, literacy upgrading time).

- Special resources and/or personnel required
  In order to improve the acculturation of an ELL, certain other support services may be required such as, bi-lingual guidance services from related ethnic associations for both a student and the family, or community service agencies.

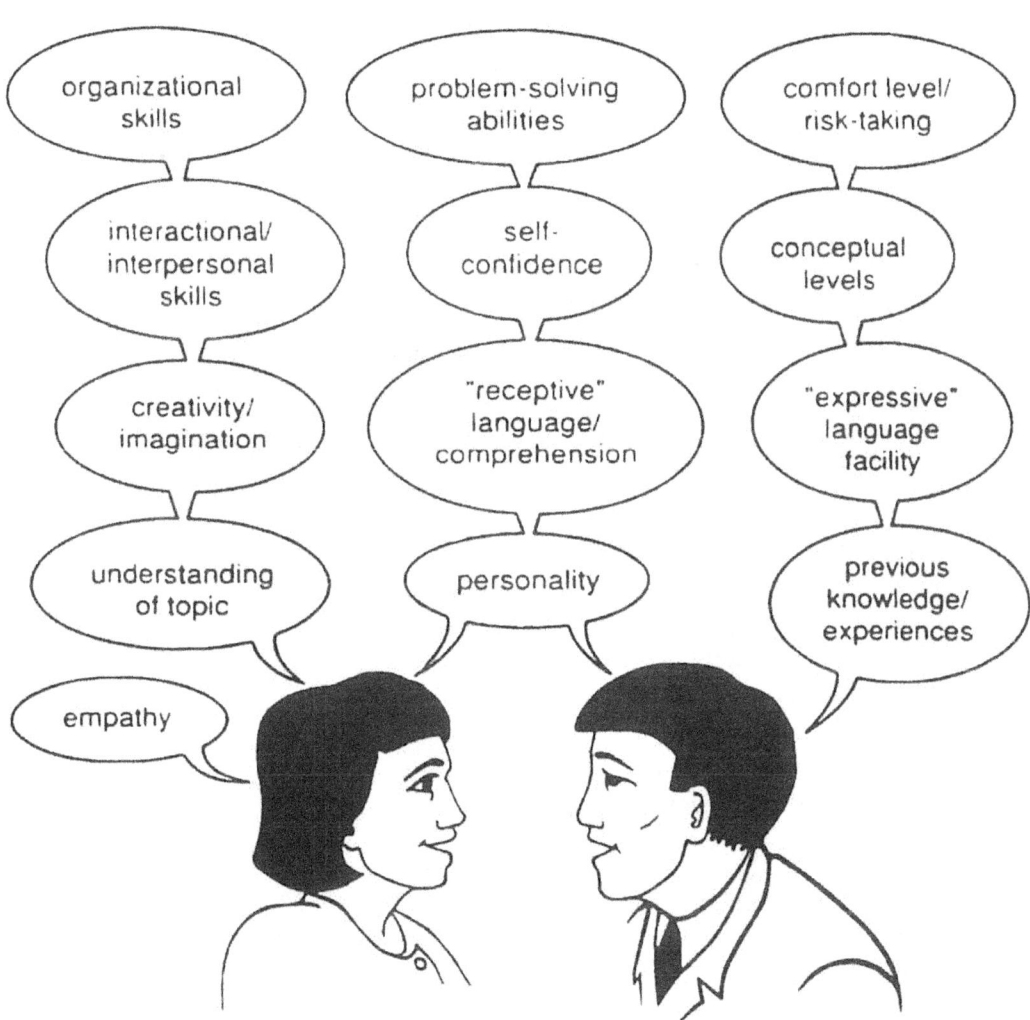

In Our Classrooms

Alternative Assessment

There's nothing so unequal as the equal treatment of unequals.
Thurgood Marshall

The following are examples of alternative assessment techniques which reduce the language barrier and allow language learners to demonstrate their comprehension, progression of skills, adjustment, and involvement.

To show comprehension, have ESL students make:

- models, dioramas
- use of drawings and illustrations
- use of translation
- time lines or other graphic organizers
- projects in first language or English or both
- a portfolio of student journal/work samples
- cloze passages, fill in blanks, and true/false tasks
- student conferencing

Also, use anecdotal notes on observation of:

- personality, preferred learning style(s), self-confidence
- a student's attempts to answer/seek information
- his/her improvement with following directions
- student speech, i.e., longer, complex sentences
- his/her involvement with lessons/seat work/peers
- a student's homework initiative
- progress from a student's previous abilities
- a student's improvement in effort and involvement
- use of free time

Remember that ESL students will understand more than they can say or write. Receptive language abilities are learned first because they are easier. Expressive abilities of speaking and writing are harder to produce. Newcomers who start at a basic level of language WILL NOT be able to write stories independently during their first year, although they could contribute ideas for a group chart story. Language learners in their third to fifth year will require support to correct and improve use of vocabulary and grammar in most written assignments.

Language Conscious Teaching
Performance Assessment of English Language Learners

> "Authentic assessment describes the multiple forms of assessment that reflect student learning, achievement, motivation and attitudes on instructionally-relevant classroom activities."
> O'Malley and Pierce, Authentic Assessment for English Language Learners

- Performance Assessment is authentic. It evaluates how a student is actively applying the language and content skills *that have been taught*. Teachers see the student making effective use of the new skills in a variety of assignments?

- Performance assessment uses criteria relevant to English language learners since progress is *referenced to the student's starting levels* in both language and literacy.

- Performance assessment *takes a longitudinal view* of a student's growth through seasons, grades and across subjects in order to compile an authentic evaluation.

- Performance assessment requires teachers to *include observational records and work sample portfolios* that demonstrate student progress in English language and literacy skills acquisition, social skills, attitudes and efforts.

- Equity policy requires assessment for ELLs to be *based on a modified curriculum (* that provides comprehensible input in content, and instruction in semantic, grammatical and linguistic skills) and the use of alternative assessment tools.

Assessment Strategies
Appropriate for Language Learners

Use a variety of the following options
in order to create a final assessment for ELLs.

- Student Response Forms
- Student Dialogue Journals
- Teacher-Student Conferencing
- Anecdotal Observation Comments
- Task-Based Performance (group work)
- Cloze Summary
- Match Information to Visual
- Question to Answer
- Yes/No and True/False Quiz
- Remediation Progress
- Task Rubrics
-

Subject Content Assessment
Assigning Letter Grades for ELLs

There is a dilemma when it comes to assigning letter marks for ELLs on report cards. Although teachers now know how long it really takes for most ELLs to develop academic proficiencies, and teachers can recognize when errors are due to a lack of language skills, many parents do not want a teacher to indicate ESL on reports, as if it were a stigma.

Authentic and Performance Assessment require teachers to include means other than test results to determine an ELL's final mark. If teachers must use a sole letter mark for a subject, they can combine letter grades from all other assessment means, and come up with an average mark. In this way, final letter marks include a broader notion of student assessment, and be true to the goals of equity in education. Discuss the following example.

Spring Term, 2006
Daniel Lee, Date of Arrival _____ Grade 8
English, Science, etc   Overall Mark - B

Assessment Means
  Subject Test Results C
  Portfolio Samples
   - Progress from Starting Point A
   - Written Work Progression from Samples B
   - Language Skills Progression A
   - Conferencing Improvements B
  Observational Records
   - Group Work Skills - B
   - Homework - B
   - Etc.

Report Card Comments for Language in Content

- ✓ is more confident and involved with class activities
- ✓ contributes ideas in group work assignments
- ✓ presents information in a variety of ways
- ✓ uses decoding skills to read new vocabulary
- ✓ can pronounce important content terminology
- ✓ uses phonetic skills to pronounce multi-syllabic words
- ✓ uses new content vocabulary in speaking activities
- ✓ is improving intonation in English speech
- ✓ uses new vocabulary in written discourse
- ✓ understands how text features help understanding
- ✓ uses visual content to assist comprehension
- ✓ is developing ability to summarize text information
- ✓ is able to use topic words in sentences
- ✓ is able to support ideas with details
- ✓ is able to form detailed paragraphs within a topic
- ✓ is using more complex sentence forms in writing
- ✓ is using different writing styles with related vocabulary
- ✓ is learning idiomatic expressions
- ✓ is incorporating different rules of formality in context
- ✓ is able to express and reference ideas in two languages

Bibliography

Avery, Peter and Ehrlich, Susan. Teaching American English Pronunciation, New York, Oxford University Press, 1995

Brown, H. D. Principles of Language Learning and Teaching, second edition, Englewood Cliffs, New Jersey, Prentice-Hall Regents, 1987

CAL Digest Series 1, Complete Collection. Washington DC, Center for Applied Linguistics info@cal.org

Chamot, A. U. Toward a Functional ESL Curriculum in the Elementary School, TESOL Quarterly. 17(3):459-471, 1983

Chamot, Anna Uhl and O'Malley, J. Michael. The Cognitive Academic Language Learning Approach: A Bridge to the Mainstreams, TESOL Quarterly. 21(2):227-249, 1987

Clegg, John. Editor, Mainstream ESL: Case Studies in Integrating ESL Students into the Mainstream Curriculum, Toronto, Multi-Lingual Matters Ltd, 1996

Cummins, Jim. Empowering Minority Students: A Framework for Intervention, Harvard Education Review. 56(1):18-36, 1986

Cummins, Jim. Bilingualism and Minority Language Children, in the Language and Literacy Series. Toronto, OISE Press, 1981

Curran, Lorna. Cooperative Learning Lessons for Little Ones, San Juan Capistrano, CA, Resources for Teachers Inc, 1990

Di Giovanni, A., and Danesi, M. The Role of the Mother Tongue in the Development of the Ethnic Child, Toronto, ON, Orbit Newsletter, OISE Press, 1988

Meyers, Mary. Myths and Delusions: English Language Instruction in Canadian Schools, in Education Canada magazine, Spring Issue, Canadian Education Association, 2006

Meyers, Mary. In Our Classrooms: An Educators Guide to Helping English Language Learners with Curriculum, revised, Toronto, Ontario, Mainstreams Publications, 2004. 416/988-3279

Meyers, Mary. Teaching to Diversity: Teaching and Learning in the Multi-Ethnic Classroom, Toronto, Ontario, Mainstreams Publications, 1993. 416/988-3279

Paulson, Christina Bratt and Bruder, Mary Newton. Teaching English as a Second Language: Techniques and Procedures, Pittsburg, PA, Winthrop Publishers Incorporated, 1976

Rigg, Pat and Enright, D. S. Children and ESL: Integrating Perspectives, Washington DCV, TESOL Publications, 1986.

Wells, Gordon. The Meaning Makers: Children Learning Language and Using Language to Learn, Portsmouth NH, Heinemann Educational Books Inc, 1986

Westby, Carol E. Learning to Talk - Talking to Learn: Oral-Literate Language Differences, 181-210, College-Hill Press Inc, 1991

www.ingramcontent.com/pod-product-compliance
Lightning Source LLC
Chambersburg PA
CBHW081847170426
43199CB00018B/2833